The Siege in Peking

Dr. Martin in siege costume,
as he arrives in New York City, October 23rd, 1900

The Siege in Peking

Inside the legations during the
Boxer Uprising by one of the besieged

William A. P. Martin

LEONAUR

The Siege in Peking,
Inside the legations during the
Boxer Uprising by one of the besieged
by William A. P. Martin

First published under the title
The Siege in Peking,
China Against the World

Leonaur is an imprint
of Oakpast Ltd

ISBN: 978-0-85706-076-1 (hardcover)
ISBN: 978-0-85706-075-4 (softcover)

http://www.leonaur.com

Contents

To

THE MEMORY OF THE BRAVE MEN

WHO DIED IN DEFENCE OF THE LEGATIONS

DURING THE SIEGE .

AND OF

THOSE WHO FELL IN THE RESCUE

THIS VOLUME IS

REVERENTLY INSCRIBED

The Author to the Reader

When I left China only a little over a month ago I had no intention of making a book. My friends, however, insist that I should put the account of my experiences during the siege into a permanent form. To me it is painful, *Infandum renovare dolorem*. But the public, more imperious than the Queen of Carthage, must be obeyed. On reaching New York in the actual costume which I wore during the siege, I called a boy to carry my packages, my son Newell having gone to the wrong station to meet me. As I was carrying a gun, the lad remarked:

"You must have been hunting somewhere?"

"Yes," said I, "in Asia, beyond the sea."

"What kind of game?" he inquired.

"Tigers," I replied—I ought to have said hyenas. He asked no further questions, and I added no explanation. The gentle reader will find the explanation in the following pages.

I have not had time to compare views with anyone who has written on the subject, nor even to verify my dates, having depended solely on my memory, and dictated my text, with all possible rapidity, to a stenographer. Trusting the reader will regard favourably the following chapters, unkempt as they are, and that he will lay down the book with the conviction with which I have written it, namely: that in the events now going on in the Far East, great issues are at stake for the church, the state, and the world.

Audubon Park, New York,
November 14, 1900

9

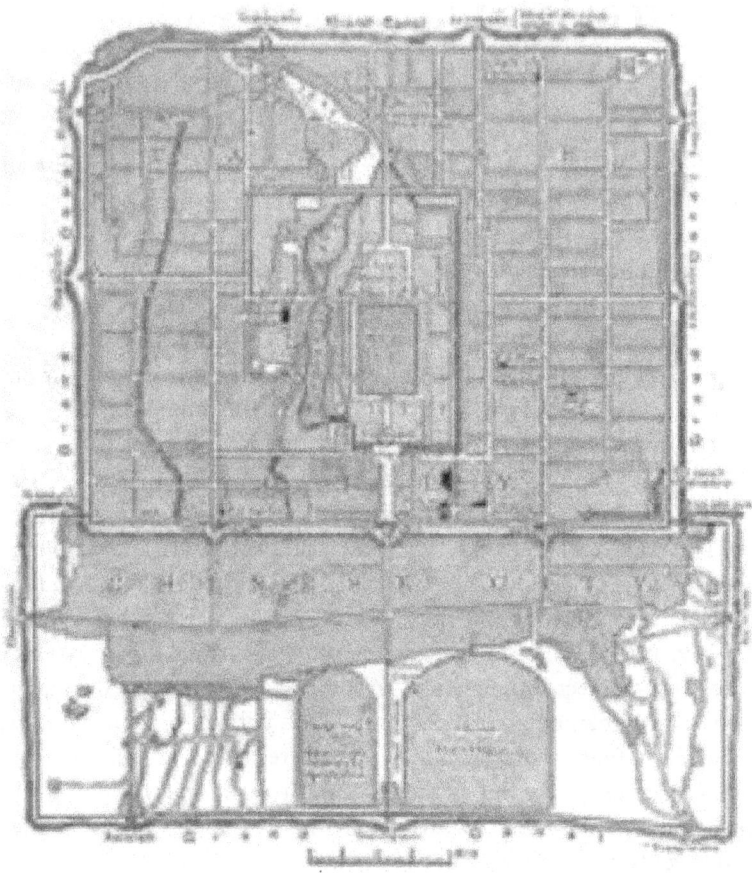

PLAN OF PEKING

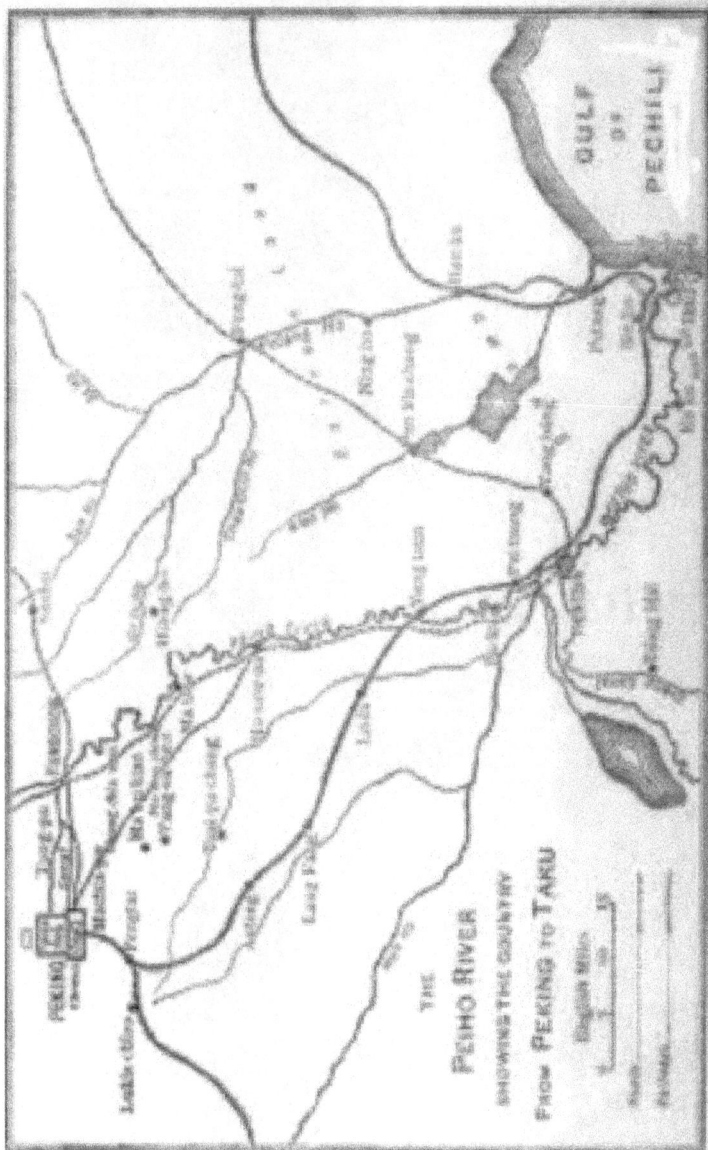

Sketch Map of the Pei-Ho River, showing the country between Peking and Taku

GORDON HALL. TIENTSIN

CHAPTER 1

The Eight Banners of the Allies and the Eight of the Manchus

Since the spring of this year the eyes of the world have been fixed on China as the theatre of a tremendous tragedy. Not only do Chinese and Tartar, prince and peasant, figure on the scene in court and camp, but many nations come on the stage in all the pomp of war. It was a magnificent spectacle, the gathering at the mouth of the Pei Ho of great navies from the ends of the earth—the storming of the Taku forts for the third time in forty years—the occupation of Tien Tsin after four weeks of continual conflict, and the advance on Peking of a combined force under the banners of eight leading powers.

Sixty years ago the British flag appeared alone in hostile array, with the result of a treaty made at Nanking, opening five ports to trade, residence, and missionary enterprise. Forty years ago the flags of Great Britain and France were united in an expedition, which opened the capital to the residence of foreign envoys, added greatly to the list of open ports, and opened up the whole country to the influence of Western ideas. Five years ago China was humbled in the dust by hitherto despised neighbours that had grown strong by the adoption of those ideas. The banner of the Rising Sun now appears along with those of seven great powers of the West, once more thundering at the gates of the Celestial Empire.

All the world asks the meaning of this unprecedented movement. What motive could be so potent as to compel those powers to bury their political animosities and to unite in one expedition? The answer is in one word, Humanity. Humanity has been outraged, and every nation of the earth either sends a contingent to avenge the wrong or sympathizes with those that send. Had America, Austria, Britain,

France, Germany, Italy, Japan, and Russia sought for a classic motto to inscribe on their banners, they could hardly find a more fitting expression of the feeling that led them to merge their several aims and rival creeds in one common purpose than the famous line of Terence, *Homo sum et nihil humani a me alienum puto*—I am a man, and nothing human is foreign to me.

Within the walls of Peking are cooped up the ministers of eleven nations (those above-named with the addition of Holland, Belgium, and Spain) along with their people to the number of a thousand men, women, and children, and menaced with the horrors of an indiscriminate slaughter. The besiegers were not, as they have been represented by Chinese diplomacy, a howling mob that had overpowered the imperial government, but an organized army under the orders of the government. Documentary evidence will be adduced in the sequel, amply sufficient to prove the complicity of the Chinese (I ought to say Manchu) Government. By making war on all who hold to principles of human progress, it has placed itself beyond the pale of civilization, and forfeited the respectable position which it formerly occupied among the nations of the earth.

If history be ransacked in quest of a parallel for the siege of the legations, it will not be found in Mafeking or Ladysmith, for Christian was there pitted against Christian. They had only to lay down their arms to insure the best of treatment. To find something akin in its savage barbarity you must go back to Lucknow, where a mixed multitude shut up in the Residency were holding out against fearful odds in expectation of relief by Havelock's Highlanders, resolved to perish of starvation rather than surrender, for the fate of Cawnpore stared them in the face.

It adds point to this parallel to remember that the Tartar rulers of China are cousin german to the Great Mogul who headed the *Sepoy Mutiny*.

It was some excuse for the King of Delhi that he was seeking to regain his throne. No such apology can be offered for the Empress Dowager of China. She has made war not without provocation, but wholly unjustifiable, on all nations of the civilized world. Allying herself with the powers of darkness, she entered into a diabolical conspiracy, and sanctioned unheard-of atrocities in order to keep her people in ignorance and to shield her family from the competition of superior light and knowledge. It is one more exhibition of the conflict of Ahriman and Ormuz, the eternal war between the spirit of darkness and the God of light.

To understand the causes of this complicated struggle, and to forecast its outcome, it may not be amiss to give separate attention to some of the parties to the conflict, especially to those that emerge from the dark cloud that rests on the Far East—the Emperor and party of progress; the Empress Dowager, and the reactionaries, the Boxers, and their associates. Three motives have combined to bring about this astounding upheaval: Political jealousy, religious antagonism, and industrial competition. The first is exemplified in the action of the Tartars, who, being an alien race, have always shown themselves suspicious of everything which tends to augment the prestige of foreigners within their territory. The second, if a fetish superstition may be dignified by the name of religion, may be seen in the obscure origin of this Boxer propaganda. The third is shown in the progress of that secret society when, transformed into a political party, it destroyed the products of foreign machinery because they interfered with the slow-going methods of an ignorant people. If the reader be impatient for the harrowing incidents of the siege, he may skip a few of the ensuing chapters; but there is reason to fear that he will not find the situation by any means as lucid as it might otherwise be made.

Curiously enough, the Tartars of Peking, like the Allied Powers, are ranged under eight banners. From the beginning of their dynasty they have been known to the Chinese as Pachi—the eight banners—ever since they passed the great wall and marched on Peking two hundred and fifty-six years ago; nor is the number of their tribal divisions the only point of resemblance worthy of notice. The errand on which they first appeared before the gates of Peking was not unlike that of our eight nationalities, *viz.: Rescue or Vengeance.*

In 1644 the city was invested by a horde of rebels led by a bloodthirsty wretch named Li Chuang. The Emperor, a Chinese of the House of Ming, knowing that resistance was hopeless, hanged himself on a hill overlooking his capital, after stabbing his daughter to the heart as a last proof of paternal affection. (How many fathers were prepared to give the same proof of affection in the extremity of our recent siege!)

Wu San Kwei, a general in command on the frontier of Manchuria, hearing the fate of his master—learning, too, that his own family had fallen into the hands of the rebel chief—called on the Manchus to aid him in the expulsion of the usurper and the punishment of his crime. On the approach of the Tartars the rebels fled, but the Tartars, on being paid off, refused to retire. It was the old story of the ass that begged a primitive man to mount his back and drive a horned stag away from his pasture-field when, to his surprise, he found himself the slave of his ally. In this case the Tartar tribes were in the saddle. Why should they dismount simply because the Chinese requested them to do so?

The tables are now turned. It is the Tartars who are chased away from the pasture-field. Foreign powers are in the saddle. Will the eight Powers whose banners now wave over the ruins of Peking be more easily satisfied? Will they withdraw at a sign from Li Hung Chang, and leave their work unfinished? In spite of diplomatic assurances to the contrary, similar conditions are sure to produce similar results. Some at least of the eight banners will be slow to abdicate their commanding position. They have put curb and bit in the mouth of the Chinese donkey, and, judging from present appearances, they are not unlikely to persist in riding the noble beast.

This and other questions as to right and policy meet us on the threshold, but we are compelled to postpone their discussion while we ask the reader to follow the eight banners of the Manchus in their occupation of China. Not only is such retrospect essential to the comprehension of recent events, for more than one lesson which might be useful to our statesmen is to be gleaned from the experience of the Manchus.

The first that suggests itself is the ease with which the Chinese may be subdued. The second is like unto it, *viz.*, the facility with which they may be governed by a foreign power. Patient, industrious, and unwarlike, they were made to be ruled by others. As a matter of fact, they have actually been under the sway (more or less complete) of different hordes of Tartars for seven centuries out of the last fifteen. From 386 to 532 of our era an extensive region in Northern China was subjected to the house of Toba. From 907 to 1234 the Kin Tartars, or Golden horde, whom the Manchus claim as ancestors, held possession of the Northern Provinces. They were displaced by the Mongols of Genghis and Kublai Khan, who extended their power to the remotest bounds of the empire, and almost at the same time brought India beneath their yoke, constituting perhaps the most extended dominion that had ever fallen to the lot of a single race. After an interval of one native dynasty the Manchus, as we have said, got possession of the throne, and they have held it from 1644 to 1900, a date which in all probability marks the end of their domination.

Instances of invasion not ending in conquest are too numerous to mention. At the dawn of history we find the Chinese, like the Egyptians, harassed by Shepherd Kings from the North. The great Wall, over fifteen hundred miles in length, hugest of tin works of man, was erected to keep them out as early as 240 B.C. When completed it was described by a historian as the *ruin of one generation, but a bulwark of safety to all that were to follow*. Would that optimistic author have pronounced such an *encomium* had he foreseen the many centuries of subjection to Tartar sway undergone by his people since that epoch?

To overrun portions of China has always been an easy task for those fierce nomads, but to retain their conquest required more than martial prowess. "I won the empire on horseback," said one of those conquerors to a statesman who besought him to encourage the milder arts.

"Can you govern it on horseback?" was the pregnant question that served for a reply.

To secure permanence of possession it has always been necessary for them to adopt the civilization (such as it is) of their Chinese subjects. By employing Chinese methods in their administration they have in many instances achieved complete success. This is the second of the important lessons suggested by their history.

The Manchus have done this more thoroughly than any of their predecessors, becoming perhaps more Chinese than the Chinese themselves; for, while the Chinese have shown themselves accessible to new ideas, the Manchus, having espoused the civilization of China, have distinctly refused to exchange it for that of the West. Yet, despite the shocking reversion to barbarism which marks the close of their history, it may be safely affirmed that no native dynasty ever governed the country with more wisdom. What they have been able to do, is it unwise for a European power to undertake?

Sir Michael Hicks-Beach is reported to have said in Parliament that "it would be madness for Great Britain to attempt the administration of any part of China."

Has not British administration converted the colony of Hong-Kong from a barren rock into the richest emporium of the Far East? Are not the Chinese, of all peoples, the easiest to govern, and are not the British confessedly the administrators of foreign dependencies? As to the possibility of a foreign power governing China, the experiment of the Anglo-French Alliance, which for a short time in 1860 governed the province of Canton through native authorities, is highly instructive; and the experience of the Manchus during two and a half centuries ought to be conclusive.

Though but a handful in comparison with their present numbers, it took them only seven years to bring all the Eighteen Provinces into subjection. Their sway began with a female Regent, as it appears not unlikely to terminate with a female Regency. The armies of the first Regent were conducted, and her Cabinet was controlled, by Ama-wang, a brother of her deceased husband. Her infant son, on ascending the throne in the first year of occupation, received the significant title of *Shunchi*, "the prosperous reign." Prosperous his reign certainly was for his people, but his enjoyment of it was brief, as he died at the age of twenty-four.

His son was the illustrious Kang Hi, who reigned sixty-one years, or a little more than a Chinese cycle, leaving behind him so great a reputation for wisdom and goodness that he was canonized by the title of "*Sheng Tsu Jin*"—sage and benevolent. Such was his avidity for knowledge that, while making himself master of the learning of the Middle Kingdom, he reached out after the sciences of the West, receiving with honour at his Court the Roman Catholic mission-aries, who a few years earlier had gone to China as pioneers of a higher science and a better faith. Not merely did he take lessons in geometry and astronomy; he appears to have been favourably disposed toward Christianity. Two things, however, inspired him with an aver-sion which he bequeathed to his successors. After having expressed an opinion as to the identity of Shang Ti, "the supreme ruler," with the Christians' God, and again as to the purely ceremonial character of an-cestral worship, he had the mortification to see his views set aside by a decree of the Pope condemning the worship of ancestors as idolatrous and forbidding, as pagan, the use of the name Shang Ti, the God of the ancient sages. What was perhaps more trying to his pride, he learned that, in order to become a Christian, he must begin by acknowledg-ing the supremacy of the Pope. Is it surprising that his writings betray a growing alienation from the teachings of the missionaries? Those teachings are condemned in one of his Sixteen Maxims, a compend of orthodoxy committed to memory by Chinese schoolboys.

His son, Yung Cheng, became, as might be expected, a bitter per-secutor of the new faith. Of Yung Cheng, who reigned thirteen years, nothing further needs to be said; though, like Julian the Apostate, in spite of his character as a relentless persecutor, perhaps for that very reason he enjoys the reputation of being a sovereign of exceptional ability.

The son of Yung Cheng was Chien Lung, the Magnificent. Happy in the possession of a submissive empire, this monarch sought to cement the ties between sovereign and subject by making frequent journeys to ascertain the state of his people. On such occasions he usually left an autograph poem (for he was no mean poet) inscribed on a granite slab to commemorate the visit. One of these effusions that I have seen at a Temple on the western hills may be rendered as follows:

Why have I scaled this misty height,
Why sought this mountain den?
I tread as on enchanted ground,
Unlike the abode of men.
Weird voices in the trees I hear,
Weird visions see in air,
The whispering pines are living harps
And fairy hands are there.
Beneath my feet my realm I see
As in a map unrolled.
Above my head a canopy
Bedecked with clouds of gold.

When he had wielded the sceptre for a full cycle he abdicated, because, as he said, it would be unfilial to surpass his grandfather in the duration of his reign. Did he not reflect how unfilial he had been in allowing himself to live longer than his father?

Kia Ching, the next in order, held the throne only half as long, and left an unsavoury name as a votary of pleasure.

His son, Taou Kwang, reigned thirty years, treading in the footsteps of Kanghi. He it was who first attempted to suppress the growing vice of opium-smoking. When the loss of revenue was employed as an argument to deter him from his purpose he exclaimed, with virtuous indignation, "Heaven forbid that I should derive profit from the vices of my subjects."

This good prince was unfortunate in the agent whom he selected to carry out his humane decree. The Viceroy Lin, haughty and overbearing, employed unjustifiable measures to obtain possession of the forbidden drug, giving just ground for reprisals on the part of Great Britain. To save himself the trouble of capturing the opium ships which lay beyond the harbour, he surrounded the whole foreign quarter at

Canton with soldiery, and threatened the lives of all foreigners, without distinction of nationality, in case of refusal to surrender the drug. Summoned by the Superintendent of Trade to deliver up as the only means of escape, the merchants handed it over to the Queen's representative to be used as a ransom for the lives of the com- munity. Her Majesty was accordingly pledged to make good their loss. To punish this high-handed proceeding, and to exact the promised indemnity were the objects of Britain's first war with China, not at all to force the Chinese either to receive opium or to consume it.

With antiquated arms, and destitute of discipline, the Chinese troops were repeatedly vanquished. Had Sir Henry Pottinger pushed his campaign to Peking, instead of signing a treaty at Nanking, he might have taken possession of the whole empire instead of the little island of Hong-Kong. The world would then have seen once more the spectacle of India and China united under the sceptre of a foreign race.

The shortest reign in the history of the dynasty was that of Hien Fung, who, ascending the throne in 1850, saw his capital in the power of foreigners at the end of a decade, and fled to Mongolia to find a grave. One of the wives who accompanied his flight was the now famous (or infamous) Dowager Empress.

Her history comprehends the reign of her son, Tung Chi, thirteen years, and that of her adopted son, Kwang Su, twenty-six years. Both will be treated in a subsequent chapter. Suffice to say, that under the Manchus, the frequent collisions with foreign powers, ranging from local riots up to serious wars, are mainly attributable to the fact that they are themselves foreigners, having got the empire by force and treachery. They suspect other nations of a desire to supplant them. Commercial ports, as they believe, are established for this purpose; religion is propagated to gain the hearts of the natives; schools and newspapers tend to render the Chinese disloyal. The privilege of carrying on these enterprises, commercial and missionary, was extorted by force, and by force it ought to be revoked. This was the advice given by a Cabinet Minister to the unfortunate Hien Fung on his accession in 1850.

"Let it be your aim," said an old counsellor—too old to learn anything new—"let it be your aim to re-establish the old restrictions all along the coast."

At the beginning of his reign Hien Fung saw his southern capital seized by the Taiping rebels, a body of fanatics who professed a sort of mongrel Christianity. Toward its end one of his arrogant Viceroys, by summarily executing a boat's crew who were sailing under the British flag, involved him in war with England and France.

Is it not strange that up to the present time the Manchus have failed to learn the futility of their attempt to expel the hated foreigners? They had been beaten by England, later by England and France together, then by Japan unaided by other powers. Is it not astonishing that they should still plan a general massacre, which was certain to provoke the hostility of all nations? Sometimes we have seen a young bull, the master of a grazing herd, resent the intrusion of a locomotive on his pasture-grounds. He places himself on the track in an attitude of defiance, but when the train sweeps by all that remains of him is a mangled corpse. Barnum's Jumbo, powerful as he was, perished miserably in making a similar attempt. Thus has it happened to the Banner men of Manchuria. Swept away by the Eight Banners of the great Powers the Manchu Government lies prostrate, and appears to be crushed beyond a possibility of reconstruction.

In treating further of this conflict between darkness and light we must draw a broad distinction between the Chinese and their Manchu rulers. The former are misguided, the latter treacherous and implacable. Among the Manchus, again, it is necessary to distinguish between a progressive Emperor and the "anti-foreign Empress Dowager". The advisers of the former in the work of reform were exclusively Chinese. The instigators of the latter in her bloody reaction were chiefly Manchus.

THE GREAT GATE OF PEKING
THIS TOWER WAS BURNED BY THE BOXERS

Chapter 2

The Emperor and the Reform Party

In the young Emperor, now in the thirtieth year of his age, reposes the only hope for even a temporary restoration of the Manchu dynasty. With features as delicate as those of a woman, and physical frame deficient in vigour, he possesses a mind singularly acute and a heart capable of being moved by the wants of his people. He alone among the occupants of the Dragon Throne during the present dynasty has exhibited a sufficient breadth of comprehension and superiority to national prejudice to desire to accommodate his government to the new civilization of the West. Stripped of power for being an ardent patron of progress, he possesses a peculiar claim on our sympathy. Nor is he to be held in any degree responsible for the outrages that have been perpetrated in his name. In fact he is rather to be regarded as himself the first victim on a long and sanguinary list.

His predecessor, Tung Chi, only son of the Dowager Empress, died at the age of eighteen in 1874. Too young to display independence of character, Tung Chi had been governed by his mother, not merely during his long minority, but she continued to exercise her influence over the policy of his government even after her Regency had been terminated by a formal proclamation.

Nothing is so well adapted to perpetuate his memory as the manner of his death. In the winter of that year a transit of Venus was to take place. More than a century prior to that date Captain Cook had made his notable voyage to the South Sea for the purpose of observing a similar phenomenon with a view to ascertaining the sun's parallax. In 1874 two American astronomers, Professor Watson of Michigan and Professor Young of Princeton University, appeared in Peking for the same object—there being no spot on the globe where it could be seen with equal advantage, and no amount of pains being deemed too great to verify our standard for measuring the magnitudes of the universe.

True to the calculated time a black spot was seen travelling across the disk of the sun. Two days later the Emperor succumbed to an attack of smallpox, or, as rumour had it, pox of a more loathsome description. Heaven had foreshadowed the event, said the people, for was not the sun the emblem of masculine Majesty? And did not the blot on the visage of Old Sol portend, or rather depict, the precise malady to which the Son of Heaven was destined to fall a victim? The popular mind became intensely excited, and the secretaries at our legation thought it advisable to smuggle the astronomers and their instruments out of the city in the gloaming of evening, with as much secrecy as possible. They had been seen erecting what looked like a battery, and mounting upon it something that had the appearance of cannon, and aiming those long tubes at the emblem of Majesty. It was inevitable that the ignorant populace should hold them responsible for the calamity which fell upon the Imperial house.

To flatter the young man's mother the doctors of the Hanlin Academy composed for him an obituary record, which made him out to be a paragon of every virtue, proposing for his posthumous title the name "*E Hwang Te*," meaning The Heroic Emperor. Yet no act in his short life has come to the knowledge of the public which suggests the idea of heroism.

The bereaved parent, resuming her Regency, cast about for a young prince to adopt, not as heir presumptive to the throne but as titular sovereign. Among the candidates available she naturally selected the youngest, like the lady who, on being asked why she had married so old a man, replied that she never had but two offers—both old—and she naturally chose the oldest. The infant chosen for this high dignity was a child of three years, the son of the Dowager's sister, and the seventh brother of Hien Fung. She gave him the reigning title of Kwang Su, meaning Illustrious Successor, and he is now in the twenty-sixth year of his reign. During one-half of that period she exercised a Regency on the ground of his immaturity, and now for a third time she assumes to exercise it on the ground of his incapacity. Well might he have merited his illustrious title had he been permitted to carry out his scheme of reform.

In her earlier days his Imperial guardian was not herself such an enemy to progress as she afterward became. As a proof of liberal tendencies may we not cite the fact that the young Emperor was early set to the study of the English language? Two of my students were selected for his instructors. Special lessons were compiled by them for his Majesty's use, and, in order to be sure of their correctness, those lessons were submitted to me. I might, therefore, plead guilty of having given some bias perhaps to the Imperial mind. Nothing is more probable than that he derived his first impulse in the direction of progress from his study of English. Yet the honour of having converted the ease-loving student into an ardent reformer is due above all others to the Cantonese doctor, Kang Yu Wei.

In Chinese scholarship the Emperor distinguished himself by uncommon proficiency. How could it be otherwise when he had for his instructors a dozen or more of the most eminent scholars of the empire! Of these the best known was the Grand Secretary, Wung Tung Ho, who specially befriended Kang Yu Wei and recommended him to the Emperor as a "thousand times more clever than myself."

A reform party is to be found in most countries, and at all times. Whether it possesses influence or not depends largely on the object toward which it is directed. In China the leading aim of the reform party was to strengthen the country by the adoption of Western methods. Unhappily, the Chinese in general were not convinced of their weakness—nor were they inclined to take institutions, the mushroom growth of yesterday, in preference to those that bore the imprint of hoary antiquity.

As early as the close of the first war with England in 1842 there were not a few Mandarins who advocated this policy on the principle, *Fas est ab hoste doceri*. For a time their efforts did not go beyond the compilation or translation of a few books, mostly historical or geographical, or both combined, with a view to acquainting China with the existence of other countries beyond her borders. One such collection, well known under the name of *Hai Kwo Tu Chi*, a description of trans-oceanic nations, was made by the unfortunate Viceroy Lin, who had provoked the war, and for having done so was sent into exile. Another, called *Ying Hwan Chi Lio*, a descriptive history of the globe, was compiled by Su Ki Yu, the Governor of Fokien Province. So frank was this Governor in expressing his admiration for foreigners and their methods that the Government, deeming him an unfit man to be intrusted with the destinies of a Province, removed him from his post and sent him into private life.

The information contained in his book he sets to the credit of the missionary, Abeel. Yet in rearranging his materials he occasionally displays a touch of originality, such as for example the statement that

Rhode Island is noted for the possession of a "colossal statue so huge that it spans the harbour and allows ships to pass between its legs."

The defeat of China in a second war in 1860 lifted this persecuted party into sudden prominence. Schools were established for the languages and sciences of the West. Youths were sent abroad for education, and poor old Su Ki Yu, by way of compensation, was made a member of the Tsung Li Yamen, the newly organized Board of Foreign Affairs. In recognition of his superior knowledge he was likewise appointed Director of the Tung Wen College, a school opened by the Foreign Board; *dans le royaume des aveugles les borgnes sont rois.* A work on the physical sciences which I prepared for the use of that school was printed at the expense of the Board, and sent forth with a laudatory preface from his pen.

About the same time Dr. Yung Wing, of Canton, a graduate of Yale College, was charged with the supervision of a select body of youth to be educated at the fountain-heads of Western learning. They were sent to Hartford in successive relays, two or three hundred in all, and continued there until they were finally recalled on suspicion of having learned too much.

Foreign legations were now for the first time established in Peking, and exercised an educational influence on the government. In this direction their first and perhaps their most important result was to induce the Chinese to send legations to the West.

Before venturing on a step so revolutionary they desired first to explore the ground. For this purpose they despatched to Europe and America the so-called "Œcumenical Embassy," headed by Anson Burlingame, who had been our first Minister to Peking. He was a man of broad views and marvellous magnetism, qualities which gave him an ascendancy over his diplomatic colleagues, leading them to adopt at that early date a "co-operative policy," which greatly resembles that so successfully advocated today by Secretary Hay. He also attracted the statesmen of China, who selected him to initiate their diplomatic intercourse with the Western world. In this embassy he was supported by two colleagues, one a Manchu, the other a Chinese, and accompanied by a number of students, mostly Manchus from the Tungwen College, who were sent abroad to complete such studies as they had begun in China.

The reform movement had thus far been confined to the acquisition of knowledge. Nothing like reform in internal administration had been attempted. A sort of reconstruction of army and navy had, it is true, been commenced, accompanied by the erection of arsenals and the purchase of munitions of war, but reform in any other sense was deemed a word of ill-omen. Their old institutions, like the Ark of the Covenant, were things too sacred to be touched.

After the ill-starred war with Japan many of the leading Mandarins, especially the junior members of the Hanlin Academy, became convinced that China required a thorough-going reformation. Reform clubs were openly established in the capital. Their members were the *élite* of the *literati*. A thrashing at the hands of a people whom they stigmatized as dwarfs and held in hereditary contempt produced tenfold as deep an impression as defeat by European powers. "Inferior to us in past ages," so reasoned these reformers, "what could have rendered these Japanese so formidable? What but the wholesale adoption of European methods, for which they have been so unjustly ridiculed. Why should not China, laying aside her antipathy, follow in their footsteps?" The expression of this sentiment created alarm at a still conservative Court. The reform clubs were not openly suppressed, but they were placed under surveillance and their name changed.

In time the work of reform was taken in hand by the Emperor himself, under the influence, as we have said, of Kang Yu Wei. It was pushed with a zeal which alarmed and astonished the empire. Innovations succeeded each other with startling rapidity. The civil service examinations were ordered to be revolutionized, a system of graded schools was to be created. The neglected children of the common people were to be gathered into schools, for the use of which the idol temples were to be appropriated. Schools for mining, commerce, and agriculture were to be established, as well as middle and higher schools of the ordinary type.

A new university was to crown this pagoda of many stages, in which the sons of the nobility were expected to acquire the science and the spirit of the modern world. The old test of fitness for office, consisting in elegance of penmanship and correctness of rhythm in essays and sonnets, was to be set aside, and in its place rigorous examinations required in sciences and practical arts. Nor did the Emperor's sweeping changes stop here. He suppressed useless tribunals, encouraged the multiplication of newspapers, and sought to bestow upon his people the inestimable privilege of free speech.

This whole scheme resembles that which has wrought in recent times such a wonderful transformation in the empire of Japan. From Japan it was in fact derived, as Kang Yu Wei himself confessed, he hav-

THE PRESIDENT AND THE FOREIGN MEMBERS OF THE FACULTY OF THE IMPERIAL UNIVERSITY.
THE SECOND FROM THE RIGHT IS PROF. JAMES WHO WAS MURDERED BY THE BOXERS.

ing insisted upon copying as far as possible the example of that country. It is, therefore, not very remotely traceable to the United States.

When Marquis Ito recently visited Peking I felt myself justified in complimenting him on the obvious fact that Japan was exerting a greater influence in the way of reform in China than any other nation, adding "much as the moon, which is our nearest neighbour, raises a higher tide than the sun, which is more remote." I fear the Marquis did not feel flattered by a compliment which implied that his country shone by borrowed light.

Though the educational scheme was outlined by Kang Yu Wei, the suggestion of the university is mainly due to Li Hung Chang. Trusted minister as he is of the Empress Dowager, he is, or has been, one of the most progressive statesmen of the empire. He it was who, during his long Viceroyalty in the North, established at Tien Tsin those schools for army and navy which have been so conspicuous in their influence on China. More than any other man he has a right to be described as a patron of modern education.

When the Rev. Gilbert Reid solicited his aid for his proposed International Institute, "Stop awhile," said Li, "you must first help me with my scheme for a university."

When the Emperor finally sanctioned the proposal it was Li who, in conjunction with another Grand Secretary, Sun Kia Nai, nominated me for the presidency.

The reformers in many instances took missionaries—notably, Dr. Allen, Rev. Timothy Richard, and the Rev. Gilbert Reid—into their counsel. Dr. Allen has led the way in Chinese journalism, and to show the effect of this wonderful awakening it only needs to be stated that, while in 1895 there were in China only nineteen newspapers, in 1898 there were no fewer than seventy-six. Mr. Richard, if not a pioneer in the diffusion of books of useful knowledge, has, following in the footsteps of Alexander Williamson, done more than any other man to promote their distribution. While at the former date the sales from the book-stores of the Useful Knowledge Society amounted only to $800, in 1898 the receipts had risen to $18,000.

The Emperor, in his wish to encourage free speech, did not confine himself to newspapers. He authorized all his officials to address him freely on the subject of reforms. To his desire to emancipate his people from the restrictions under which they had always laboured he owes his downfall.

A junior member of the Board of Rites, which has the superintendence of education and religion, had prepared a memorial on desired reforms in those departments, submitting it first to the chiefs of the Board. They refused to forward it to his Majesty. The Emperor was enraged that they should dare to intervene between him and any of his progressive officials. He deprived them of office. Those old conservatives, burning with shame for their disgrace, hastened away to the country palace and threw themselves at the feet of the Empress Dowager, imploring her to resume her Regency in order to save the empire from the furious driving of this young Phaëton, who was in danger of setting the world on fire. She listened to their prayer, and, striking him as with a thunderbolt, entered upon her reactionary career. She began by requiring him to address to her a humble petition confessing his incapacity and imploring her to teach him "how to govern his people."

Kang Yu Wei and some of his associates, being warned by the Emperor, made good their escape, but six of them were brought to the block, and many others followed at no great interval. The programme of reform was blotted out with the blood of its advocates. This was the *coup d'état* of August, 1898.

Exit Emperor—enter Empress Dowager.

Chapter 3

The Empress Dowager and Her Clique

This is the third time the Dowager has come on the stage in the character of Regent. May not the young Emperor reappear once more in the character of reformer, clothed with a portion at least of his former authority? What an opportunity was thrown away when the foreign Ministers in Peking declined to uphold him, and allowed an ambitious woman to reverse the direction of his policy. Yet they ought not to be censured for maintaining the role of passive onlookers—the *coup d'état* having been effected without great bloodshed, and without any pre- monition of the disastrous convulsions for which it prepared the way.

In 1860 they committed a worse blunder by reinstating this same woman, who then, as now, had fled from an invading force, and aiding her in the suppression of a more magnificent reform. I allude to the Taiping rebels. Imbued with principles borrowed from the religion of the West, and established at the southern capital, where they were easy of access, those insurgents, if favoured by foreign nations, would have shown themselves amenable to good influences. Paganism would have been swept away, and with it a permanent cause of conflict with Christian powers, while a vigorous native power would have been set up in place of an old decaying dynasty of foreign origin.

A still better thing might have been for England and France to divide China at that epoch, and forestall the complications attendant on the greater number of claimants who are now competing for power, influence, or territory. On some of these questions opinions may differ, but in view of subsequent events there is no room to doubt that it would have been good policy to sustain the Emperor in his attempt to renovate the empire. Instead of a capital in ashes, and a nation debased to barbarism, what an impetus would have been given to all kinds of improvement and what horrors would have been averted!

The best apology for want of foresight is that the Chinese themselves appeared to acquiesce in the usurpation. It was in appearance only, as we afterward learned from sundry appeals on behalf of the Emperor, as well as from threats of rebellion in case of violence to his person. Diplomacy, with all its vaunted skill, is at best a succession of happy (or unhappy) accidents, a series of blind attempts to penetrate the future. Of Him who holds in His hand the *arcana* of destiny is it not said *that He maketh diviners mad*? Not only were our diplomatic representatives unable to see within the veil; by the usage of nations they were precluded from abjecting to a change of administration which had the appearance of being acceptable to the people.

Before proceeding with our narrative a retrospect of the Dowager's romantic and eventful career will not be out of place. One piece of romance originating some five years ago in a New York Sunday paper may at once be pricked with the needle of truth. I refer to the story of her being originally a Canton slave-girl—presented to the Emperor by one of his Tartar generals who had returned from that city. Her family is well known in Peking. Her brother, lately deceased, was Duke Chao. Her sister married a younger brother of Hien Fung, and if further proof were required I may add that Dr. Pritchard, an English medical missionary, being called in to prescribe for the ducal family, was asked to bring with him his wife, and on that occasion both he and Mrs. Pritchard had the honour of being served with tea by the hand of a venerable white-haired lady who was mother of the Empress Dowager.

Outside of the family of Duke Chao, the Dowager has an extensive connection, embracing subdivisions of two or three of the Eight Banners. Some years ago she received them all as her family relatives, *sans ceremonie*, at a temple near the great East Gate. In the palace she was Empress, and very few of them were high enough to be admitted to her presence. Here she was one of them, and she made them feel that the ties of kindred were not forgotten. Justice requires that we should chronicle this good trait in a woman who since then has shown herself to be such a monster of iniquity.

Before she was twenty she became secondary wife of the Emperor Hien Fung, and had given him an heir to the throne. His consort being childless he was overjoyed by the birth of a son, and, to signalize his satisfaction, he raised the young mother to equal rank with Consort No. 1, assigning her a palace on the west not inferior to that of her colleague on the east.

Beautiful, gifted, and well educated, she adorned her new position. When in 1861 it came to a joint Regency, *Tse An*, "the daughter of peace," was quite eclipsed by her brilliant colleague, *Tse Hi*, "the daughter of joy." In the previous year they had both fled to Tartary with their lord on the approach of the allies. Whether the stubborn Tse Hi prompted him to fly rather than submit, it is impossible to determine; but such a course would not have been out of keeping with what we now know of her obstinate, unyielding character. Had her character been different would she not have taken warning by her former *hegira*, and made peace in good time to save her capital?

On that occasion she was the leading spirit in the joint Regency; with Prince Kung, brother of her deceased husband as Prime Minister, a post which he won by taking the lives of two other princes, as he gave out in order to preserve that of the infant Emperor. Her recent flight was, therefore, not her first. Is it not remarkable that she should live to repeat the experience after a lapse of forty years? Instead of being taught caution in the school of adversity she seems to have been emboldened and embittered.

At a summer palace rebuilt for her use on the Hill of Longevity, overlooking the beautiful Kwenming Lake, she had before her the spectacle of the ruins of the Yuenming-yuen, the most sumptuous abode of Oriental majesty, where she had dwelt in the heyday of youth—it was too costly for an impoverished government to undertake its restoration—nor did the view tend to propitiate her feelings toward the authors of its destruction. Here, on the borders of the lake, she lived in nominal retirement on laying down her second Regency some fifteen years ago, but never for a day did she cease to concern herself in affairs of state, or to exert political influence through the medium of the Emperor. Was he not her adopted son? Did he not owe his elevation to her choice? She was resolved that he should not forget these obligations, and, by way of keeping them in mind, she required him to visit her once in five days at the distance of fifteen miles, and to knock his head or perform the *kotow* at her feet.

At all times a power behind the throne, the part he took in administration was clearly indicated in a decree that appeared some months before the *coup d'état*, in which the Emperor requires all great officers throughout the realm to render thanks for their appointment to the

Dowager as well as to himself. He had never ceased to consult her in regard to such appointments. Was it not natural that, on returning to power, she should require him to issue a decree inviting her to "teach him how to govern"?

In the eyes of most of her subjects her intervention was not merely justifiable—it was imperative. She was not known as conservative in any objectionable sense. Had she not led the way in encouraging, or at least permitting, her people to learn the arts of the West? After forty years of experience, was there any danger that she would adopt an opposite policy? She herself denied that she was actuated by hostility to progress. Said she, in an edict explaining her position: "When we have been choked it does not follow that we are to cease eating, merely for fear it may happen again."

She meant to say that the Emperor had crammed his reform down the throats of his subjects with dangerous haste. She only wished to give them time to digest their aliment.

In another edict she forbade any further search to be made for the accomplices of Kang Yu Wei, because, as she said, she abhorred the shedding of her people's blood. It is not surprising that the world was led to credit her with a degree of amiable humanity as well as prudent moderation. How insincere were her professions in both utterances will appear from the intemperate zeal which she soon displayed in undoing what had been done by the Emperor, and in pursuing the alleged conspirators.

These tendencies were not at once apparent, especially as her past record was such as to inspire confidence. This time, however, she had taken the reins into her hands with the avowed intention of undoing the Emperor's work. Reversing the engine (to change the figure) the train began to move on the back track, slowly at first, but gradually attaining a furious velocity that rendered a smash-up inevitable.

This tendency was not perceived by some of the Emperor's most trusted Ministers. The High Commissioner Sun, for instance, when a few days after the *coup* I called on him with a list of nominations to chairs in the new university, declined to take action until he should have an audience with the Dowager, not knowing whether he might not himself be dismissed from office or subjected to some heavier penalty. A few days later, satisfied on this point, he sanctioned them all and assured me there would be no change of policy as to the educational programme.

Marquis Ito had just arrived from Japan, attracted no doubt by the

Emperor's professed desire to copy the example of that island empire. Our High Commissioner and the Metropolitan Prefect united in giving him an entertainment, inviting Li Hung Chang to meet him. They also invited me as president of the university—the only Occidental present on that occasion. The conversation turned wholly on the subject of reform in Japan. The Marquis related how, returning from his studies in England over thirty years ago, he was asked by the Prince of Chosiu if he thought it would be needful to change anything in the political or social life of Japan. "Yes," he replied, "everything must be changed."

So successful had he been in effecting reforms in Japan that it was hoped he might be retained in Peking as adviser for a moderate course of reform in China, such as might be carried out without provoking a revolution. He had not come with any such expectation. Needless to say, his advice was not sought for by the reactionary government.

Reactionary measures began at length to appear in the Official *Gazette* by heaps and clusters. The old examination system for the civil service was confirmed. The creation of common schools was countermanded. The Bureaus of Mines, Commerce, and Agriculture were suppressed. Official sinecures were restored.

Almost the only progressive institution left standing was the new university. Whether this was due to Li Hung Chang having been its advocate, or to Yung Lu becoming its protector, or to both, certain it is that it appeared to be in no danger of suppression at the hour of the outbreak. New buildings were in process of erection, and the appointment of new professors authorized up to that very date. Time-serving censors had denounced it, but Yung Lu came forward to defend it, saying that "to suppress the university would be a disgrace in the eyes of foreign nations."

In the way of social progress a very striking innovation took place, under the direct influence of the Empress Dowager. For her it was a master stroke of policy, filling the ladies of the legations with delight and securing their powerful influence in her favour. In former years they had never been received at Court, but the Dowager now thought fit to intimate her willingness to receive them.

The Emperor at the beginning of the year received the Ministers, as he had always been wont to do, to present the congratulations of the season. They found him taciturn, depressed, and apparently suffering in health. What wonder, when he was no more than the shadow of his former self, serving then, as he has continued to do, for a mere pictorial representation of majesty.

Being a woman, the Dowager, with all her self-assertion, did not venture to call the Embassadors into her presence. Such proceeding would, without doubt, have resulted in a counter revolution producing an earthquake shock throughout the empire. In lieu thereof she thought she might arrive at the same object by admitting the ladies of the legations. Perhaps, too, she was not entirely free from being influenced by feminine curiosity. Those who were invited did not fail to accept, nor had they any reason to decline, as thus far the Dowager had not in any way betrayed her savage nature.

She treated them with most engaging condescension, and bestowed a little souvenir on each—a talisman to cherish kindly sentiments and bind them to her party. The ladies described her manners as charming, and her appearance, done up as she was, as that of a woman of thirty, though she was then not far from sixty-five.

So far from displaying anti-foreign sentiments in the formation of her policy, the Regent took pains to conciliate foreign powers. Of this, a striking proof was the readiness with which she yielded to the demand of the French Minister that the privileges of official rank in the Mandarinate should be granted to Roman Catholic missionaries according to their rank and standing in the church.

In domestic affairs she had, it is true, begun to persecute the party of reform, and to pursue its leaders with relentless severity. For this her excuse was that they had plotted against her—an excuse abundantly valid according to Chinese precedent; for any such action on their part constituted treason in the eyes of the administration.

It is believed that her suspicions were not ill-founded; that the young Emperor, prompted by his advisers, had even despatched General Yuen with secret orders to take the life of the Viceroy Yu Lu, a main supporter of her cause. On the way to Tien Tsin he suddenly changed his mind, and, instead of the point of a *poniard*, he presented the Viceroy with the reverse end of an arrow which he carried as symbol of his commission to take the Viceroy's life. By his defection the success of the *coup d'état* was assured. He has accordingly since then been one of the Dowager's trusted favourites, and now holds the high office of Governor of Shantung.

The hints sometimes thrown out that in her earlier years she had arrived at undivided sway, first by disposing of her lord and then by setting aside his consort, are unworthy even of refutation, nor is it to be credited that she had any designs on the life of the young Emperor, whom she found it so convenient to employ as a tool. He serves her for a figure-head, and in his name she has put forth her most objectionable decrees. Had she put him out of the way she must have found it necessary to adopt a successor. This she was able to do without the perpetration of such a crime. The Emperor, being childless, she announced at the beginning of this year her decision to adopt as son, and successor to her son, the son of Prince Tuan, grandson of an elder brother of Hien Fung.

This lad, Pu Chun by name, was fourteen years of age, in the direct line of succession, and nothing would be easier than to have the Emperor abdicate in his favour as soon as she might deem it desirable to do so.

The adoption of the great Aga, as the heir to the throne is familiarly called, raised his father, previously almost unknown, to sudden prominence. Personally Prince Tuan seems to have been in the confidence of the Dowager, and since then he has controlled her counsels, while in relation to all the grandees of the empire he has enjoyed the prestige inseparable from one who is father to a reigning monarch—so soon was Pu Chan expected to succeed to the Dragon Throne.

That which appeared to bring about an unfavourable change in her foreign policy was the occurrence of repeated aggressions on her territory by foreign powers. When Germany obtained the cession of Kiao Chao, under circumstances which will be explained in the next chapter, Russia at once insisted on being permitted to occupy the seaport of Port Arthur as terminus for her Siberian railroad. England, always on the alert to check the advance of the Northern power, demanded a seaport on the opposite side of the Gulf of Pechili. France, unwilling to be left out in the cold, asserted her pretensions as the equal of any of the great powers, and in the name of the balance of power insisted on obtaining the seaport of Kwang Chao, between Canton and her Annamite dependencies. Italy, too, scoured the coast of Chekiang in quest of a convenient port to occupy.

At each step in this series the haughty Regent became more infuriated, ordering that preparations should everywhere be made for resisting invasion, and openly expressing her will that in case of any attempt to encroach further on Chinese territory she would engage in war, no matter which or how many powers might be concerned. At this juncture the Boxer agitation hove in sight, and she welcomed it as a heaven-sent auxiliary.

That movement now claims our attention, and with it the fate of the Dowager is inseparably bound up.

Never has her character been so much discussed as during this, her third Regency. She has been compared to Elizabeth of England and to Catherine of Russia, but, in my opinion, for her the fittest prototype is Jezebel of Samaria, who slaughtered the prophets of the Lord, and rioted with the priests of Baal.

CHAPTER 4

The Boxers and Their Allies

Those Boxers are not, as represented, a new body called into existence by the missionary work in China. They are, on the contrary, an old association, a kind of Masonic order, which attracted the attention of the Government more than a century ago.

In 1803 they were placed on the index as a prohibited association by the Emperor Kia Ching, on account of their tendency to cause trouble in the state. They originated in a some- what benighted corner of Shan Tung, and after this interdict they languished in obscurity until they were quickened into life by contact with Europeans. Their creed takes its shape—

If shape that may be called which shape has none
Distinguishable in member, joint or limb—

from a blending of the three religions of Buddha, Laotse, and Confucius, together with all sorts of popular superstitions. They profess certain mysteries of their own, such as hypnotism, and to this they owe the fascination which they exercise over the ignorant. Meeting with susceptible persons they employ them as mediums, and through them in a state of trance they obtain communications from their gods. Many of them possess the power of throwing themselves into this abnormal state at will. In drilling for war all their soldiers (for the most part very young persons) are expected to do this, as well as to practise pugilism and other antics. I have myself seen them drilling, though I did not venture to remain long enough in their midst to take photographs with a camera.

Riding in the street one day, a lad apparently of sixteen ran across in front of my horse, threw himself on a bank, and went into a trance. I was tempted to wait to see what would follow, but, reflecting that on coming out of this hypnotic state he would probably attack me and so bring on a riot, I thought it prudent to move on. On the eve of an encounter they kneel down and bow themselves toward the southeast, which is the direction from Peking of Southern Shan Tung, where they originated. Having invoked the protection of their gods, accompanied by hocus-pocus forms, they believe themselves invulnerable; a belief no doubt due to the fact that in a hypnotic condition they are insensible to outward impressions, and no longer conscious of pain.

When recently Catholic missionaries penetrated their stronghold, a collision was inevitable, and two of them, Germans by nationality, were murdered. This provoked the intervention of the Kaiser, who not only exacted the execution of three of the murderers but profited by the occurrence to get possession of a seaport in that quarter.

The people of the province were greatly excited, not so much perhaps by territorial aggression as by their opposition to railway lines, which the Germans commenced laying out. In many instances they tore up the track and attacked the engineers. The Boxers became at once transformed from a Masonic fraternity into a great political organization. Their propaganda spread like wildfire. Bands of youths were to be seen undergoing their mysterious discipline in every hamlet, nor were they confined to the stronger sex.

A special branch was created for the young women of the province—a feature the more remarkable on account of the jealousy with which Chinese women are ordinarily kept in seclusion. One of their war-songs commences thus:

> We, the brothers of the Long Sword, will lead the van;
> Our sisters of the Red Lantern will bring up the rear guard.[1]
> Together, we will attack the barbarians,
> And drive them into the sea.

Their designation of Brothers of the Long Sword is due to the patronage afforded them by Yu Hien, a Manchu Governor, who, desiring to oppose the Germans in their railway enterprise, found the fittest instruments among these fanatical Boxers. Calling them into his Yamen he had them perform in his presence, and, becoming apparently convinced of the reality of their pretensions, he distributed

1. If anyone doubt that Chinese women are easily infected by a martial spirit let him consider the fact that the Taiping rebels formed female brigades, as these later fanatics have done. An extremely popular ballad, called Mulon the Maiden Chief, affords evidence of the same thing. See Appendix.

among them a number of long swords, the only weapon for which they expressed a wish.

They were not long in learning to use them. Not only were railway engineers and missionary stations attacked, but Christian villages were everywhere laid waste. The foreign representatives at Peking demanded the removal of the Governor, and he was replaced by Chang Yao, a Chinese general who proceeded vigorously against the Boxers, making it so hot for them that they crossed the boundary into the neighbouring province of Chilhi, where Peking is situated, and where the Manchu viceroy was known to be their friend.

Chang Yao's fidelity to his commission gave offence to the Court, and he was in turn replaced by the time-serving Yuen, who in many instances has shown himself capable of playing a double part.

Yu Hien, on arriving at the capital, was decorated with a breast-plate bearing the monogram for "Happiness," written by the elegant pencil of the Dowager herself, meaning no doubt that he had been the happy discoverer of an auxiliary force. He was then transferred to the Governorship of Shan Si, where he has since imbrued his hands in the blood of more than fifty missionaries. At his instance the leaders of the Boxers were called to the capital and admitted to the palace of Prince Tuan, father of the Heir Apparent, who, on seeing their performances, became himself a convert, and has since continued to be their ardent patron.

The Dowager, at Tuan's suggestion doubtless, allowed them to give her an ocular demonstration of their supernatural powers. She also seems to have had her doubts dispelled, if she had any, as from that moment she gave them free scope, and took good care that none of her officials should put any obstruction in their way. This hypothesis, and no other, can account for her readiness to stake the life of her dynasty on the success of the Boxers.

Unglaube du bist nicht so viel ein Ungeheuer,
Als Aberglaube du!

(Of the twin monsters, unbelief and superstition, the more monstrous is superstition, exclaims a German poet.)

General Nieh, a Chinese who commanded the forces of the Metropolitan Province, having killed some of the Boxers, was visited with a severe reprimand. The Viceroy, desirous of keeping on good terms with foreigners, despatched troops against them. Having had instructions from the Empress he took good care that his troops should fire over their heads or employ nothing but blank cartridges. None of the Boxers were killed. Their pretensions to invulnerability won credence among the people. Vast numbers flocked to their standard, and they moved on like a devastating flood, sweeping away every Christian community that lay in their track. Two English missionaries were killed not far from the capital. One had been killed in the Province of Shan Tung. How many Catholic missionaries were slain I am unable to say, but the number of converts destroyed by their merciless foe was estimated by Bishop Favier at not less than thirty thousand.

The course of their march was steadily in the direction of Peking, for, although edicts were from time to time issued forbidding their advance, they were always secretly encouraged to go forward—the double-faced Dowager menacing them with one hand, to please the foreigner; and beckoning them with the other, to please herself and Prince Tuan.

The cause of the Boxers was helped by a widespread belief that the year would be unlucky because the Eighth Moon would be intercalary. Twice in five years a month is duplicated, making thirteen in the year. It is not, however, unlucky unless it be the eighth, which is not a matter of choice.

I may here add a reference to the calendar which is not superstition, but statistical. According to the *North China Herald*, out of thirty-four anti-foreign riots that have taken place, fourteen have occurred in the month of June. This was announced by way of warning in April or May, and the frightful outbreak at the capital makes fifteen in the same month. For this enormous preponderance I can offer no reason unless it be due to the frequency of drought at that season, in conjunction with the orgies of a three-days' festival.

One or two specimens of the manifestoes issued by these Boxers will serve to show their *animus*. One which was extensively placarded in Peking began thus:

"For forty years the foreigners have been turning the empire up-side down. They have taken our seaports, got possession of the administration of our revenues [referring to the Customs service], and they do despite to our gods and sages."

To most of their proclamations they prefix the motto, *Uphold the Great Pure Dynasty, and destroy the ocean barbarians.*

To curry favour with the government they took the name of volunteers, and came to be recognized as patriots, although they had no hesitation in ravaging the towns and destroying the property of their countrymen, who were not in any way connected with foreigners. If called to account for so doing, they could always defend themselves on the ground that those people were consumers of foreign goods.

The new recruits by whom their ranks were swelled belonged mostly to the labouring classes, and here the third motive comes into play. Some were boatmen, whose lumbering craft lay rotting on the banks of the Pei Ho, because they had been superseded by steam navigation. Some were conductors of caravans or drivers of wagons, thrown out of employ by railway transportation. Letter-carriers (for China has had a rudimentary postal system for many centuries) also joined the hostile host, because they found themselves thrown out of service by new postal arrangements—the slow transmission of intelligence by foot or mounted courier being superseded by the telegraphic wire. Finally, workers in metals and weavers on hand-looms came in crowds to reinforce a body which proposed to destroy the products of Western machinery. The peasantry, too, were far and wide induced to espouse the same cause, not by a fear of competition, but by a long-protracted drought, which made it impossible to sow their fields or gather their crops. They were made to believe that heaven had withheld its rain, either through the diabolical arts of foreigners or by being offended at their presence, and that the blood of those foreigners alone would propitiate the gods.

The following specimen, of which thousands of copies were scattered at Tien Tsin, is peculiar in the prominence assigned to Buddhism:

SACRED EDICT.

ISSUED BY THE LORD OF WEALTH AND HAPPINESS

The Catholic and Protestant religions being insolent to the Gods and destructive of holy things, rendering no obedience to Buddhism and enraging both Heaven and Earth; the rainclouds no longer visit us, but 8,000,000 Spirit Soldiers will descend from Heaven and sweep the Empire clean of all foreigners. Then will the gentle showers once more water our lands; and, when the tread of soldiers and the clash of steel are heard, threatening woes to our people, then the Buddha's Patriotic League of Boxers will protect the Empire and bring peace to all.

Hasten, then, to spread this doctrine far and wide; for, if you gain one adherent to the faith, your own person will be ab-

solved from all future misfortunes. If you gain five adherents to
the faith, your whole family will be absolved from all evils; if
you gain ten adherents to the faith, your whole village will be
absolved from all calamities. Those who gain no adherents to
the cause shall be decapitated; for, until all foreigners have been
exterminated, the rain can never visit us. Those who have been
so unfortunate as to have drunk water from wells poisoned by
foreigners should at once make use of the following Divine
Prescription, the ingredients of which are to be decocted and
swallowed, when the poisoned patient will recover:

Dried black plums	half an ounce.
Solanum dulcamara	half an ounce.
Liquorice root	half an ounce.

If it be asked what were our Ministers in Peking doing all the while,
that they adopted no effective measures to avert the coming danger, I
answer they were, one and all, not insensible to appeals which reached
them from without. Yet they never for a moment suspected that there
was any real danger of an insurrection in the capital.

On that point official information from the Chinese Government
outweighed the representations of missionaries. Turning a deaf ear to
the Cassandra prophecies of the latter, they allowed themselves to be
soothed by the siren song of the former.

"Those Boxers," said the Mandarins, "are not soldiers. They
only practise a sort of innocent gymnastic with a view to the
protection of their own homes. Sometimes, indeed, they get
into disputes with their Christian neighbours leading to bloodshed, but they are an undisciplined rabble, who cannot make
head against the military. The Dowager Empress will at once
issue orders for them to disperse and return to their homes."

As to the comparative safety of Peking I was myself as much astray
as any of the Ministers, for I wrote to my relations that I thought the
capital in no danger, as it was patrolled by a well-organized military
force. "Peking," I said, "is the safest place in China."

For not foreseeing the rising in the capital one Minister is not
more blameworthy than another, yet may the French Minister fairly
be held culpable for neglecting to take effective measures to stay the
scourge which destroyed the flourishing missionary work carried on
by his countrymen. Had he seized the Chinese gun-boats, and laid an

embargo on the seaports of China, the government would soon have been brought to its senses.

Though apprehending no sudden outbreak, the diplomatic body still thought it prudent to demand permission to introduce a guard of marines for their several legations. The Yamen objected, and parleying went on for some weeks. At length, on the 27th of May, the railway to Paoting Fu was torn up, the station-houses burned down, some of the employees killed, and others put to flight.

Taking alarm for the first time, the Ministers decided to proceed without the consent of the Yamen. The guards were sent for, and they arrived (about four hundred and fifty including officers) not an hour too soon, for the next day the other branch of the track was also destroyed, and communication with the sea-coast completely cut off. This was the beginning of the siege.

THE PAVILION ENTRANCE TO THE BRITISH LEGATION, WHERE ALL THE FOREIGN MINISTERS WITH THEIR FAMILIES, TOOK REFUGE.

CHAPTER 5

Siege of the Legations in Peking

This siege in Peking will undoubtedly take rank as one of the most notable in the annals of history. Others have been longer. The besieged have been in most cases more numerous, their sufferings have oftentimes been greater, yet this siege stands out uniquely as the uprising of a great nation against the whole of the civilized world. Cooped up within the narrow bounds of one legation—the British, which covered the largest area and contained the largest number of buildings—were people of no fewer than fourteen nationalities and the Ministers of eleven nations, the whole number of foreigners not much short of one thousand, and having under their protection about two thousand native Christians. Outside of the city gates, somewhere between the city and the sea, was an army under the banners of the eight foremost powers of the world advancing to the rescue, and the eyes of the world were fixed on that movement with an intensity of interest which no tragedy has ever awakened in the spectators of the most moving scenes of a theatre.

All the appliances of modern civilization contribute to this effect. The telegraph has flashed the news of our distress beneath the waves of the ocean, and the navy yards and camps in the four quarters of the earth are set in commotion. The politics of nations give way to the interest of the universal public in the one great question of the possibility of rescue. From day to day the daily papers chronicle now the advance, then the retreat of the rescuing party. Hopes and fears rise and fall in alternate fluctuation. At one time the besieged are reported as comfortably enjoying themselves, protected and well fed; at another they are represented as having been massacred to a man with all imaginable attendant horrors. It is our object in this chapter to present its successive phases as they actually occurred, without going back to discuss preliminary questions.

The siege divides itself into two distinct stages. During the first of these, of only ten days' duration, the Boxers are our conspicuous enemies, the Government and soldiers of the Chinese Empire keeping themselves studiously in the background. In the second stage, which lasted eight weeks, the Government and its soldiers come prominently forward, and the Boxers almost disappear.

The guards summoned for the eight legations were not over four hundred and fifty, including officers, yet they saved the situation. Had they been delayed no more than forty-eight hours the whole foreign community in Peking must have perished, for reliable rumour affirmed that the Boxers had resolved to attack the legations and destroy all foreign residents during the midsummer festival, which occurs early in June. Without that handful of marines defence would have been hopeless.

Rumour (in this case also reliable) further affirmed that the Empress Dowager had resolved to give the Boxers a free hand in their conflict. Should they succeed, so much the better. Should they fail, there would still be room to represent (as Chinese diplomacy has industriously done) that the government had been overpowered and its good intentions thwarted by the uprising of an irresistible mob.

Rumour further asserted that, by way of clearing the ground for their operations, the Empress Dowager had given consent to the complete destruction of the quarter of the city occupied by the foreign colony, *viz.*, a street called, from the number of legations which are situated on or near to it, "Legation Street," together with numerous blocks of Chinese buildings to a considerable distance on either side.

On the 9th of June, buildings and property belonging to foreigners in the southern, or Chinese, division of the capital were destroyed by fire. Foreigners, whether missionaries or civilians, living at outlying points in the Tartar city took refuge under their respective national flags. Missionaries brought with them their flocks, small or great, of native converts, who were equally exposed to the rage of their enemies.

All possible measures were preconcerted for defence. Notice of our peril was flashed to the sea-board by a roundabout route, and it was hoped that we might maintain ourselves for a few days until the promised relief should arrive. A strong body of marines, led by Admiral Seymour and Captain McCalla, set out from Tien Tsin by rail, intending to repair the road, not knowing how much it was damaged, and hoping to reach us in two or three days. That hope proved illusory, for week succeeded week, during which we were encouraged by fictitious reports of their advance, while in reality they had been driven back upon their base and the destruction of the railway completed. Had they in the first instance abandoned the railway, and pressed forward across the remaining interval of some forty miles, they might perhaps have succeeded in reinforcing our Legation Guards, placing our community in security, and perhaps they might have averted the subsequent declaration of war; but I am anticipating.

A larger expedition was being organized by the admirals of the combined squadron at the mouth of the river. On the 19th of June a circular from the Yamen notified the foreign Ministers that their admirals had demanded the surrender of the forts (they did not say had carried the forts by storm, which was the fact), adding, that "this is an act of war. Our country is therefore at war with yours. You must accordingly quit our capital within twenty-four hours accompanied by all your nationals." Exit Boxers—enter the regular Chinese army.

Thenceforward we were exposed to all the force the Government could bring against us.

Warned by a kind letter from Mr. Squiers, Secretary of the American Legation, offering me the hospitality of his house, I had previously there taken refuge from the university, where I had been living alone at a distance of two miles. While we remained in the United States legation no direct attack was made upon us by firearms, but we were in hourly danger of being destroyed by fire, or trampled down by a rush of the Big Swords.

The fires of which I have spoken as having first shown themselves in the outer city were not confined to mission chapels. A large quarter, containing the richest magazines of foreign goods and estimated to be worth from five to ten millions of pounds sterling, was laid in ashes by the infuriated Boxers, not merely with a view to ridding themselves of industrial competition: perhaps also in the expectation that a fair wind would carry the conflagration over the walls and destroy the foreign settlement.

As a matter of fact the high tower overlooking the great central gate of the Tartar city caught fire and was consumed. The firebrands fell in profusion on the inside of the walls, and we all turned out in expectation of having to fight the flames. Happily a change of wind rendered this unnecessary.

Within a few days conflagrations were kindled by the Boxers them-

Scene of Baron Von Ketteler's murder.
Archway on Ha Ta Men Great Street

selves in the inner city—missionary chapels, school-houses, churches, and cathedrals were wrapped in flames, and lighted the lurid sky night by night for a whole week.

The new, or northern, cathedral, standing in an open ground by itself, was considered as not incapable of defence. Monsignor Favier bravely resolved to hold it at all hazards, and thus preserve the lives of three thousand converts who had there taken refuge. In this he was aided by a volunteer band of forty brave marines, French, Italian, and Austrian, together with a disciplined force of native Christians. The defence of that cathedral forms the most brilliant page in the history of the siege.

It was not, however, until the siege was raised that we had any conception of the severity of the conflict that devoted band had to wage in order to keep the enemy at bay, for from us, though separated only by an interval of two miles in a direct line, they were cut off from communication as completely as if they had been situated at the North Pole.

After the declaration of war and the ultimatum above referred to, the Ministers had a meeting, at which they agreed that it would be impossible to comply with the demand of the Chinese Government. They resolved to request an extension of time, or at least to gain time by parleying over the conditions until our expected relief should arrive. With this view they agreed to go separately to the Yamen to make remonstrance against the harsh treatment implied in this ultimatum.

On the 18th two Boxers, mounted in a cart, had ostentatiously paraded the street, by way of challenge, as heralds were wont to do in feudal times. As they passed the German legation the Minister ordered them to be arrested. One made his escape; the other was captured and brought round to the U. S. legation. On consultation it was decided to keep him a prisoner, and he was led away, the Baron giving him a sound beating with his heavy cane.

On the morning of the 20th Baron Ketteler set out for the Yamen, in pursuance of this arrangement. No sooner had he reached a great street than he was shot in the back, falling dead immediately. His secretary was at the same time wounded, but succeeded in escaping to a mission hospital, whence, after his blood was stanched, he was carried back to his legation.

The news produced a panic in all the legations. They considered that the projected massacre had begun, and, as the British legation alone was regarded as capable of defence, to that they fell back, accompanied by all their nationals. Sir Claude MacDonald had generously placed its resources at the disposal of his colleagues.

Had the enemy followed up their advantage and poured into the outlying legations (abandoned as they were) they might have reduced them to ashes, or, pursuing us into that of Great Britain, they might have overpowered us in the midst of panic and confusion. Happily they were held in awe by their opinion of foreign prowess, and carefully abstained at that time from coming to close quarters. In the course of the day, it was found that the legations had not been invaded by the enemy, and they were reoccupied by their proper guards with the exception of the Belgian, Austrian, Dutch, and Italian, which lay beyond the line of defence, and were, speedily destroyed by fire.

Baron Ketteler's life was in no unimportant sense a ransom for many, but his was not the only foreign life offered up that day. In the afternoon Professor James, of the Imperial University, while returning from the *fu* of a Mongol prince on the opposite side of the canal, was shot dead in crossing the bridge. He, too, sacrificed his life in a noble cause; for he, along with Dr. Morrison, of the *London Times*, had there made arrangements for the shelter of native Christians.

That very evening, and thenceforward every day, we were fired on by our besiegers. The fusillades were particularly fierce when a thunderstorm occurred, the Chinese seeming to regard heaven's artillery as coming to supplement the use of their own weapons.

The most dangerous of their attacks were, however, made with the firebrand. Numerous buildings beyond our outer wall were successively fired for no other object than to burn us out. Of these the principal was the magnificent palace of the Hanlin Academy, containing the most costly library in the Chinese Empire. That library only served the ruthless vandals for the purpose of kindling a conflagration, and manuscripts of priceless value, dating back five or six centuries, were consumed by the flames or trodden under foot. By almost superhuman effort the flames were subdued and the enemy driven back. That building henceforward became a bloody battle-ground between the contending forces, which at times approached so near each other that the enemy assailed us by throwing kerosene oil, and our people replied with oil of vitriol in hand-to-hand encounters.

Early in this part of the siege a struggle occurred which more than any other was the pivot of our destiny. This was on the wall. It had been held by Chinese soldiers, but, dominating all the legations, had heavy artillery been there planted, defence would have been impossible. The Chinese were driven back from a portion of it by a combined force of Americans and Germans; but, returning in greater numbers, they gradually forced our troops to abandon their position. The situation appeared desperate. The Germans being insufficient in number to defend their own legation, a combined force of Americans, British, and Russians, amounting to about sixty men, was organized under the lead of Captain Myers, of the United States marines.

Before the onslaught which was to decide our destiny Captain Myers pronounced a remarkable harangue. Pointing to the British legation, "My men," he said, "yonder are four hundred women and children whose lives are dependent upon our success. If we fail, they perish, and we perish also. When I say go, then go." The Americans and English must have been moved beyond expression by this appeal. The Russians, too, though they knew not a word of his speech, fully comprehended the meaning of his gesture. They, as well as the others, were willing to offer their life's blood for the success of this forlorn hope.

The Chinese, taken by surprise, were driven from their barricades, and a large space fronting the legations remained in possession of our foreign guards. But the victory cost us dear, for, besides several others killed and wounded, the gallant leader who deserves to be regarded as one of the heroes of the siege fell wounded to the ground. Thenceforward he was unable to take that share in our defence for which his soul thirsted.

Within the legation all was bustle and activity. The marines, reinforced by a volunteer corps of a hundred or more, were occupying commanding points on the legation walls, or making sorties from the legation gates—sometimes to capture a gun which threatened to breach our defences, sometimes to disperse a force that was gathering for an assault. Night and day this went on, week after week, but not without loss. Several of the leaders of these sorties fell in not abortive attempts, and many of their soldiers were wounded. Our fortifications were strengthened partly by sand-bags that were made to the number of many thousands by the ladies, who incessantly plied the sewing-machine—an instrument which on that occasion proved to be no less effective than our machine-guns.

Much work was also done in the way of digging trenches to countermine the operations of the enemy. Most of this was superintended with great skill by missionaries, whose merit has been frankly acknowledged by diplomatists and generals. It was carried out by the bone and muscle of native Christians. With regard to these unhappy

A PORTION OF THE WALL OF PEKING HELD BY THE ALLIES

refugees, who were destitute of home and livelihood, it has also been acknowledged that without their aid the defence would have been impossible.

Surely, in the final settlement, the losses of the native Christians should not be left out of view, nor should precautions be neglected to secure their safety in the future.

For eight long weeks we were sickened by hope deferred. The forces of our defenders were weakened by daily losses. Our store of provisions was running low. Had the rescue been delayed another fortnight we must have suffered the fate of Cawnpore, rather than the fortune of Lucknow. We had eaten up all our horses and mules, to the number of eighty! Only three or four remained, affording meat for not more than two days. Our meal barrels had also reached the bottom, and unhappily the widow's cruse of oil was not within our reach. Our clothing even (we had many of us no change of raiment) was worn to shreds, and it became unfashionable to appear with a clean shirt.

This reminded me of a few lines from a well-known poet, referring to another city, which I had written in my notebook on my first visit to Peking, forty-one years ago. (They are a photograph of the city as it then was. And now its condition is tenfold worse.)

Whoso entereth within this town
Which sheening far celestial seems to be,
Disconsolate will wander up and down
'Mid many things unsightly to strange e'e.
For hut and palace show like filthily;
The dingy denizens are reared in dirt;
Nor personage of high or low degree,
Doth care for cleanness of surtout or shirt
(Childe Harold.)

If asked how we spent our time, I answer, there was no time for amusement, and no unseemly frivolity. Fear and anxiety dwelt in every bosom, but we took care that they should not show themselves upon our faces. Especially did our brave women strive to look cheerful in order to strengthen the arms of their defenders. In the midst of the fiercest attacks, when rifle-shots were accompanied by bursting bombs, only one gave way to hysteric shrieks (she was not American); and it may be added, by way of offset, that one man, a Norwegian, went stark mad.

The place was overcrowded, and such was the want of room that forty or fifty from the Roman Catholic missions were domiciled in an open pavilion, where some of them were wounded by stray shots. Of Protestant missionaries, forty-three were lodged in the legation chapel. The chapel was employed, I need hardly say, more like a hotel than a meeting-house. There was no time for praying or singing. Sunday was as busily devoted to fighting as week days, nor did I once hear of a prayer-meeting. Yet never was there more heartfelt praying done than during this trying period.

Within the British Legation I was transferred from the table of Mrs. Squiers to that of Mrs. Conger, both families occupying only a part of the small house of the legation doctor. Had I been her brother I could not have been treated with more affectionate kindness than I received at her hands and those of the Minister. Calm, resolute, hopeful, and, as Pope says, "Mistress of herself, *though China fall*," a devout Christian, too, though tinged with the idealism of Bishop Berkeley, Mrs. Conger is one of the most admirable women it has been my privilege to know. I wished many a time that, like her, I could look on all those events as nothing more than a horrid nightmare, merely conjured up by a distempered imagination. The round shot by which our walls were pierced was too tangible to be resolved into fanciful ideas. The United States has had in Peking no worthier representative than Major Conger. A soldier through all the War of Secession, he met this outbreak with a fortitude and good sense pre-eminently conspicuous. A man of broad sympathies and deep insight into Chinese life and character (especially after the experience of the siege), it is well that he has been intrusted in a large measure with the negotiations looking to a final settlement.

Some incidents of the siege may here be introduced.

First among them was the fall of the British flag, not in the order of time, but in the impression which it made upon our minds. Charged with the duty of inspecting the passes of Chinese coming and going between the legations, my post was at the gate over which it waved so proudly (and there, through the whole siege, I passed my days from 5 a.m. until 8 or 9 p.m.). Never did it wave more proudly than during those days when, beneath its ample folds, it gave asylum to the ministers of eleven legations and to people of fourteen nationalities. Never was the pre-eminent position of Great Britain more conspicuous—a position in keeping with her history in the opening of China, and the paramount influence which she has exerted on the commerce and politics of that empire. One day, in the early morning, down came the flag, the staff having been shot away. We had observed that for several days it had been made a target for the enemy. The Chinese seem to take as reality what to us is no more than poetry in speaking of the protection of a flag. With them the flag is supposed to be accompanied by a guardian spirit. In this case they would call it the tutelar genius of the British Empire.

Before going into battle they offer a sacrifice to their own banner. If they are able to seize, or in any way; destroy, the banner, of their enemy, they consider the battle as more than half gained. To us the fall of the flag had the effect of ill-omen. It was not replaced for a number of days, and the aspect of the gate-tower, deprived of its glorious crest, was certainly depressing. When replaced it was not exalted to its former height—the flag-mast being purposely shortened in some degree to guard against a repetition of the misfortune.

On one of the first days of my service at the gate-house a marine belonging to the guard there stationed was shot down, and died instantly. Where the shot came from it was not easy to determine, but on all sides, at no great distance, were trees and high buildings in which it was possible for sharpshooters to conceal themselves. So much, indeed, were we apprehensive of unseen messengers of death that at night we seldom lighted a lamp, taking our dinner before nightfall, and when lamps required to be lighted they were always extinguished as soon as possible, not to attract the aim of hidden marksmen who might at night occupy commanding positions which would be too dangerous for them during the day. Let it not be supposed that, because the Chinese are backward in the military art, they were deficient either in weapons of precision or in the skill to use them. Let the fate of our captains and their men be the answer.

One British captain, Halliday, was grievously wounded in a sortie. His successor, Captain Strouts, was shot dead in crossing the canal in front of our gate. Captain Wray was shot in the head, but not killed, in attempting to capture a gun. The captain of French marines was killed. He had complained, a few weeks earlier, that in Peking he had nothing to do and that the marines had been summoned on a false alarm. The wound of Captain Myers (and how he got it) has already been mentioned.

The sad procession closes with Captain Riley, of the United States Navy, who in the hour of occupation, while playing his artillery on the palace gates, fell a victim to a sharpshooter. It would seem, indeed, as if those sharpshooters, as in other lands, knew how to pick off the officers at the head of their troops, yet so numerous were the casualties among our men as to show that their attention was not confined to officers.

As rifle-shots were parried by our high walls, our chief danger was from cannon. With these the enemy appeared to be insufficiently provided, but gradually one after another opened its Cerberean mouth until big guns and little guns were barking at us on all sides. The most dangerous gun was that of which I have spoken as aimed at our wall from the distance of a few yards. The expedition for its capture was not successful in accomplishing that object, yet so frightened were the Chinese soldiers by the daring of that attack that they thought fit to remove the precious piece of artillery to a safer distance, and its roar was no more heard.

Guns of heavy calibre were erected on the northeast of the Fu, which played havoc with the French and German legations, and almost daily kept us awake by the explosion of shells over our heads. Guns of less weight were placed on an angle of the Imperial City wall, close to the British legation. They commanded both sides of the canal, and threatened to demolish a flimsy fort hastily thrown up for the protection of our gate.

Hitherto we had nothing with which to respond larger than a machine-gun. The want of heavier metal was deeply felt, and one of our marines, Mitchell by name, aided by an ingenious Welshman named Thomas, undertook to construct a cannon out of a brass pump—putting two pieces together and wrapping them with steel wire somewhat as Milton represents the devils as doing in the construction of a cannon out of a hollow pine. Before it was completed, however, Sir Claude forbade its use, saying that to keep the pump to meet a possible conflagration was of far more vital importance.

Luckily, while this work was going on, the gunners were informed by a Chinese that in an old junk-shop within our lines they had discovered an iron cannon of considerable size. It was brought in, and so good was it that they resolved immediately to rig it up for use. Examination proved it to be Chinese, though at first it was supposed to be of English make.

Mounted on an Italian gun-carriage, and provided with Russian bomb-shells, it became useful to us and formidable to our enemies. The Russians, though bringing ammunition, had forgotten their gun. The Italians, I presume, had found theirs too heavy, and brought the empty carriage. Put together and served by American and British gunners it was not unfitly christened the International. It led the way in many a sortie, prostrating barricades, and frightening the enemy by its terrible thunder. Not, however, being a breech-loader, and the ammunition being ill-adapted, it was inconvenient to handle.

In one of these sorties, Mitchell, the brave gunner, who seemed to love it as if it had been his sweetheart, had his arm shattered.

The first shells that began to rain upon us led us to apprehend a heavier shower, and to contrive umbrellas for our protection. These so-called "bomb-proofs" were in reality excavations made in the ground in front of the building occupied by each legation. They were barely large enough for the women and children: the men were expected to stand outside to fight the enemy. They were covered over with heavy beams, and these again with a *stratum* of earth and sand-bags. No cavern in a hillside could look more gloomy or forbidding. The first rain (not of shot or shell) filled them with water, and we said to our ladies that, in order to avail themselves of these laboriously constructed bomb-proofs, they would have to put on their bathing-suits.

The ladies were not timid, and were not therefore in haste to try the virtues of a mud-bath. To some of them, the bursting of shells and crackling of small arms, if not music, was yet not without a stimulating effect. On the first shots Miss Conger, who was suffering from nervous prostration, threw herself into her father's arms and wept convulsively. At the next attack she bore the ordeal with perfect composure. As the siege went on, the daily fusillades appeared to act upon her nerves like a necessary tonic. She grew stronger from day to day, and at the end of the siege she seemed to have obtained a complete cure, a thing which she had sought in vain by an ocean voyage.

In the Conger family were three ladies from Chicago, who, having their visit cut short by the outbreak, on going to the railway station found the road broken up, and returned to have their visit prolonged by the siege. Mrs. Woodward went about everywhere, even in places of danger, armed with her camera, but her post of constant service was in the hospital, where our wounded boys affectionately called her by the name of "Mamma." Many other ladies, professional and unprofessional, worked hard to nurse those brave fellows back to life. Her handsome young daughter, if she rendered any service besides the sewing of sand-bags, did it chiefly by inspiring certain young men to heroic deeds. The mother having expressed to me a wish to have a Boxer's rifle for her museum, I whispered in the ear of young Bismarck, who the next day brought the desired weapon, and, laying it at her feet, said, "This is the spoil of an enemy whom I shot this morning."[1]

The other lady, Miss Payen, was a skilful painter in water-colours, and her elegant art, though slower than the camera, has no doubt contributed to preserve memorials of the siege not a few.

These three ladies were a powerful reinforcement to the three ladies of the Conger family, and the six attracted not merely young men, but had frequent visits from such old men as Sir Robert Hart and the Spanish Minister, Mr. Cologan, a *hidalgo* of Irish extraction.

No man kept up his spirits better than Sir Robert, who was always cheerful, and his conversation sparkled with humour, notwithstanding the Customs head-quarters and Imperial post-offices, erected and organized by him as the visible fruit of forty years of service, had all been laid in ashes. On arriving in the legation he said to me, "Dr. Martin, I have no other clothes than those you see me standing in."

As we looked each other in the face, we could not help blushing for shame at the thought that our life-long services had been so little valued. The man who had nursed their Customs revenue from three to thirty millions, the Chinese were trying to butcher; while from my thirty years' teaching of international law they had learned that the lives of Ambassadors were not to be held sacred!

He was accompanied in this place of refuge by Mr. Bredon, Assistant Inspector-General, and all the Customs staff, as well as by the professors in the Tungwuen College, and I was accompanied by seven of the professors in the Imperial University—one having fallen a martyr to his good works. All these co-operated with the missionaries, and others, in discharging various duties, the humblest of which was made honourable by the circumstances of the siege.

Some spent their days in digging trenches, others inspected latrines in the interest of sanitation. One of our professors superintended the butchery of horses and the distribution of horse meat, while a Commissioner of Customs presided over the operations of a Chinese laundry.

In the way of food-supply the greatest service was rendered by a Swiss named Chamot. Only an innkeeper, his name will be recorded on the roll of fame, and the French Minister proposes to procure

---

1. It would be unfair to overlook Miss Pierce, a fair niece of the Congers, under whose inspiration Dhuysberg, a young Dutchman, performed more than one exploit. In a word, all our men were doubly brave because they had our women to encourage them.

for him the cordon of the Legion of Honour. To us he was *Corvus Elia*, the raven of the prophet Elijah, bringing us bread morning and evening, but (what a pity!) no meat. He had newly opened a hotel, which, aided by his brave wife, who carried a rifle and used it with effect, he fortified and defended. He opened a flour-mill for the occasion, and kept his bakery running at high speed to supply bread (sour and coarse it was), barely sufficient for a thousand mouths. As he crossed the bridge, often was he fired on, his bread-cart was pierced by many bullets, and once his flag was shot away.

I recall a notable expedition in which Chamot and his bright young wife bore a conspicuous part. After the burning of the churches several parties were sent out to bring in the surviving Christians. One of these parties was accompanied by Chamot and his wife—she discharging the full duty of an armed soldier.

Another of these parties proceeding to the Nan Tang southern cathedral was accompanied by Dr. Morrison, a man equally skilled with gun or pen, and no less brave in the use of the latter. His opinions are worth a broadside of cannon.

On this occasion he went at the instance of Mrs. Squiers, and was accompanied by Professor James, who acted as interpreter. Mrs. Squiers is a woman of large heart and long purse, whose feet were never weary in looking out the abodes of the poor and needy.

When this last company of refugees came in I saw them in the street before they proceeded to the Fu. Never had I witnessed such a heart-moving spectacle. Two hundred of the forlornest objects I ever beheld had been raked up from the ashes of their dwellings. Starving and weary, they seemed scarcely able to stand. They were old and young, men and women, all apparently ready to perish. One woman was the mother of Ching Chang, a student of mine, former Minister to France. She, like the others, was on foot, and equally destitute of all things. Her family has been Christian for many generations.

The object most striking to the eye was a man of fifty bearing on his shoulders his mother, a white-haired woman of threescore and ten.

In the Fu were domiciled near two thousand of such fugitives, of whom four or five hundred were Protestant. The latter were subsequently removed to other quarters.

The Fu was, as I have said, defended by Austrians, French, Italians, and especially by the Japanese, at the cost of much bloodshed, though assailed by the heaviest guns and the fiercest forces of the enemy. Its importance came from its covering the approach not only to the four legations—Spanish, Japanese, German, and French—beyond the river it also commanded the canal front of the British legation. To this (in part at least) our Christians owed the protection of their asylum.

In these engagements more than half the Japanese, under the lead of Colonel Shiba, were killed or wounded, and many of the other nationalities. Daily some were brought through the gate only to die in the hospital. Often have I saluted bright young soldiers as they passed out, and seen them return in a few hours dead, dying, or maimed for life.

Never had I so vivid an impression of the vanity of human life.

Oh, Great Eternity,
Our little life is but a gust
Which bends the branches of thy tree,
And trails its blossoms in the dust.

Yet never was the thought of death less pleasant to my mind—not that I feared to die, but that I abhorred the thought of perishing in an indiscriminate massacre of men, women, and children. My feeling was like that of the weary woodcutter who, laying down his load, exclaimed with a sigh, "Oh, Death, when wilt thou come?"

Instantly the Angel of Death appeared before him, asking: "You called me. Why?"

Frightened by the aspect of the grizzly terror the woodman answered, "Only to help me take up my burden."

So I, though over threescore and ten, was persuaded by the same apparition to bear my burdens a little longer.

Within our walls but few were killed or wounded by shot or shell. The health of the imprisoned community was remarkably good, perhaps the better because they had to live on low diet. The only deaths from disease were those of small children, who, deprived of milk and exposed to heat, withered away like flowers; no less than six of them within a few short weeks filling infant graves.

Ordinarily in Peking the heat of summer is unendurable, and every foreigner escapes to the mountains or the sea. On this occasion

God tempered the wind to the shorn lamb.

The heat was not excessive for a single day, yet what Holmes calls "*Intramural aestivation*" as far from agreeable. Our experience was true to the picture given in that amusing skit:

His ardent front, the cive anheling wipes
And dreams of erring on ventiferous ripes.

We all lost flesh from perspiration and want of food—some ten, some twenty, some fifty pounds. A Frenchman, apparently to make my apprehension more clear than by using the metric system, drew out his coat to exhibit the yawning vacancy which ought to have been filled by a well-lined stomach.

After the siege not a few strong men were brought down by fevers produced no doubt by the privations of that trying time.

My post was a vantage-ground for observation, and one of the deepest impressions made upon me was by seeing men of all nationalities passing to and fro co-operating for the common weal. It presented a foretaste of that union which, we trust, may be realized in the coming millennium, with this difference, that then the nations shall "learn war no more." The lines of creed and nationality appeared to be obliterated. An orthodox Russian priest filled sand-bags or dug trenches side by side with a Roman Catholic or Protestant missionary. Often did I converse with the Catholic missionaries of France, and I felt myself irresistibly drawn to them by their spirituality and devotion.

Having heard of the approach of the army of relief, we became more cheerful. Two ladies asked for my autograph, to be inserted in *A Cycle of Cathay,* and I wrote *Juvabit meminisse* (It will be pleasant to remember). The next day, the French Minister, who was noted for the gloomy view he had always taken of the situation, came to the gate and said to me, "*Eh bien, nous sortirons d'ici*" (We shall get out of this). "*Juvabit meminisse*"—alluding to the inscription.

That we were able to hold out was, perhaps, in some degree due to divided counsels amongst our enemies; for we learned, with deep sorrow, from the Court Gazette, which had been surreptitiously brought in, that four ministers in the Tsung Li Yamen had been executed by order of the Empress Dowager. We mourned them as our friends, who had employed their influence as far as possible in our favour. Of this I feel assured, for one of them was the High Commissioner for Education, who had the supervision of our new university. Two others were directors of the Tungwen College, the diplomatic school of which I was president for so long a time, and I had come to hold them in the highest estimation. One of them had sent three of his sons to be under my instruction in the new university.

Prince Ching undoubtedly exerted a powerful, though secret, influence in our favour.. Commanding, as he did, the City Guard, a Manchu force of fifty thousand men, had he chosen to let them loose upon us all at once, we must have been inevitably overwhelmed. Though he lacked the courage to remonstrate with the tyrant Empress, he had the power and the tact to restrain the fury of his soldiery.

One of our greatest privations was the want of newspapers. Not merely were we without intelligence from the great world beyond the sea, we were for the most part in absolute ignorance as to what was going on outside of our own walls. From time to time we sought to remedy this state of things by endeavouring in one way or another to get a glimpse, by means of messengers let down at night, as Paul was in a basket from the wall of Damascus, or by purchasing intelligence from our enemies.

In this last way Colonel Shiba considered himself peculiarly fortunate in finding a man who gave him daily intelligence of the approach of our relief. One day they had reached Lang Fang; another, they had got to Chang Kia Wan, and, after passing five or six stations, it seemed as if they were just about to reach Peking, when he felt it necessary to turn them about and make them fall back a stage or two in order to keep up the flow of remuneration. He was paid some thirty dollars a day for this cheering news. Needless to say that for the whole of it he had drawn on his imagination.

One of our messengers who was most successful, having succeeded in the guise of a blind beggar in reaching Tien Tsin and bringing back most encouraging letters, was a lad of sixteen. Though not a Christian, he had begged to be taken under the protection of a Christian mission, and nobly did he reward their kindness by his intrepidity. Having sewed the letters between the soles of his shoe he was three times searched without discovery.

On August 14th, after midnight, a sentry burst into our sleeping-room, calling aloud:

"They are coming!"

The Minister and myself arose and rushed out into the open air, not requiring time to put on our clothes, for we had never put them off. True enough, we heard the playing of machine-guns on the outside of the city. Never was music so sweet. We awakened the ladies. They also listened. The news spread from one building to another, until all were under the open sky listening to the playing of those guns, as the women at Lucknow listened to the bagpipes of Havelock's Highlanders. Overwhelmed with joy, some impulsive ladies threw themselves on each other's necks and wept aloud.

The next morning, at ten o'clock, the great gates of the legation were thrown open, and in came a company of mounted *Sikhs*, perhaps the finest cavalry I ever beheld, and with their long spears and high turbans they appeared the handsomest men on whom my eyes had ever rested. So, perhaps, by the magnifying effect of time and circumstance, they appeared to all of us as the vanguard of the army of relief. They had come in through the water-gate, by which the passage would have been impossible but for the occupation of the wall by our marines.

The rest of our troops, of various nationalities, entered later in the day by the great front gate, the key of which Mr. Squiers, acting as Chief of Staff to Sir Claude MacDonald, had captured from the flying enemy. He, too, is one of the heroes of the siege. Many others there are whose names I cannot here mention, though they deserve to be recorded indelibly on the roll of fame.

Deeply sensible of the difficulties attending the march on Peking, and knowing, as I did not then, the cost in precious lives which that expedition for our rescue required, I have no words sufficient to express my admiration or my gratitude. Let me close by the expression of one wish, namely: that those forces will not be withdrawn until full security is obtained against the recurrence of a similar outburst of pagan ferocity.

The day following we did not forget to express our thanks to a Higher Power; meeting in the open air, where, after the reading of *Te Deum Laudamus* by the British chaplain, Dr. Arthur Smith pronounced a discourse, in which he pointed out ten particulars showing the finger of God in our rescue. He might have extended them to a hundred.

ASSAULT OF THE RELIEF COLUMN ON OUTER WALL OF PEKING FROM A JAPANESE PAINTING

Chapter 6

Additional Incidents of the Siege

A few more incidents which appear to be worth recording are, for obvious reasons, here given in a separate chapter.

Among the Roman Catholic missionaries, one white-haired father especially attracted my attention. I had seen him walking on the bank of the canal amidst a shower of bullets, apparently courting death, yet in words he expressed the hope of rescue.

The morning of our deliverance he grasped my hand, and, looking up with streaming eyes, exclaimed: "*Te Deum, Te Deum, Laudamus.*" Setting off alone without escort to carry the good news to the Bishop at the northern cathedral, he was shot dead *en route* by some enemy in ambush. Mr. Knobel, the Netherlands Minister, was wounded in the same way the day after the siege was raised, while standing on a bridge near the legation.

In the batch of Peking *Gazettes* referred to in the former chapter as brought in surreptitiously, there were several decrees of considerable interest. One of them referred to the murder of the Japanese *Chancelier* on the 11th of June. He had gone to the railway station in the hope of getting news of Seymour's relief column. He was there set upon by soldiers and Boxers combined, dragged from his cart, and slain. This being nearly a week prior to the capture of the forts, the Empress Dowager, wishing still to shun responsibility, issued the following decree:

On hearing this intelligence we were exceedingly grieved. Officials of a neighbouring nation stationed in Peking ought to be protected in every possible way. Now, especially, should extra care be taken to prevent attacks upon them, when desperate characters swarm on every side. We have repeatedly commanded the various local officials to concert measures for their protection, and yet, in spite of our orders, we hear of the murder of the *Chancelier* of the Japanese legation here in the capital of the empire.

Our civil and military officers had been anxiously clearing their districts of bad characters. We now order all the Yamens concerned to set a limit of time for the arrest of these criminals, that they may suffer the extreme penalty of the law, etc., etc.

A coloured print, extensively circulated in Shanghai and elsewhere, depicts this event with a view to firing the loyal heart, representing the murder not as the act of a mob, but as an execution by court martial, with Boxers drawn up in one file and soldiers in another; the whole presided over by General Sung, a high commander of the Imperial forces.

On June 21st, two days after the declaration of war, the Dowager sent forth a manifesto, in the name of the Emperor, for the purpose of announcing her action and justifying it to her subjects:

Ever since the foundation of the dynasty, foreigners coming to China have been kindly treated. In the reign of Tao Kwang and Hien Fung they were allowed to trade, and to propagate their religion. At first they were amenable to Chinese control, but for the past thirty years they have taken advantage of our forbearance to encroach on our territory, to trample on the Chinese people, and to absorb the wealth of the empire. Every concession made only serves to increase their insolence. They oppress our peaceful subjects, and insult the gods and sages, exciting burning indignation among the people.

Hence the burning of chapels and the slaughter of converts by the patriotic braves. (Scil. Boxers.)

The throne was anxious to avoid war, and issued edicts enjoining protection of legations and pity toward converts, declaring Boxers and converts to be equally the children of the state. This decree we issued in hope of removing the old feud between our people and the native Christians. Extreme kindness was shown to the strangers from afar, but these people knew no gratitude, and increased their encroachments.

A despatch was yesterday sent by them calling upon us to deliver up the Taku forts into their keeping. Otherwise they would be taken by force. These threats are a sample of their aggressive disposition in all matters relating to international intercourse. We have never been wanting in courtesy, but they, while styling themselves civilized states, have acted without regard for right, relying solely on their military prowess. We have now reigned nearly thirty years, and have treated the people as our children, while the people have honoured us as their deity. In the midst of our reign we have been the recipient of the gracious favour of the Empress Dowager. Furthermore, our ancestors have come to our aid. The gods have answered our call, and never has there been so universal a manifestation of loyalty and patriotism.

With tears have we announced in our ancestral shrines the outbreak of war. Better it is to do our utmost and enter on the struggle than to seek self-preservation involving eternal disgrace. All our officials, high and low, are of one mind. There have also assembled, without official summons, several hundred thousands of patriotic soldiers (Boxers). Even children carry spears in the defence of their country.

Our trust is in heaven's justice! They depend on craft and violence. Not to speak of the righteousness of our cause, our Provinces number more than twenty, our people over four hundred millions. Surely it will not be difficult to vindicate the dignity of our country, etc., etc.

The document concludes by promising rewards to those who distinguish themselves in battle, or subscribe funds, and threatening punishment to those who show cowardice or act with disloyalty.

On June 24th the Board of Revenue is ordered to give Kang Yi two hundred bags of rice as provision for general distribution among the Boxers. A decree of the same date appoints one of the princes to be the official head of the Boxer organisation. It says:

Our people included in the Boxer organisation are scattered all over the regions around the metropolis and Tien Tsin. It is right and proper that they should have a Superintendent placed over them. We therefore appoint Prince Chuang (a first cousin of the Emperor) and the Grand Secretary, Kang Yi, to be in general command of the said society. We also order Brigadier-Generals Ying Nien and Tsai Lan to act in co-operation with them.

All the members of the Boxer Society are exerting their utmost energy, and the Imperial family must not fall behind in its efforts to take revenge upon our enemies.

Nothing could show more distinctly the complicity of the government in the Boxer movement—and its responsibility for the outrages perpetrated by the Boxers—than these documents. Yet our admirals, in demanding the surrender of the forts, took care to announce their purpose as that of coming to the aid of the government against the Boxers!

About the middle of July a white flag, or rather a white sheet of paper, was displayed on the upper bridge, announcing to us, in large letters visible with the aid of a telescope, that "we have received orders to protect the Foreign Ministers."

The same day, a small supply of melons, vegetables, and flour were sent in to us, accompanied by overtures for an armistice, and proposing that Princes Tuan and Ching should be admitted to an interview. The melons and fruits were eaten with gusto, but the flour was shunned as probably not conducive to health. The proposed meeting with the Princes was conceded, though regarded with suspicion, on the principle,

Timeo Danaos et dona ferentes.

But when the time came, they failed to appear, excusing themselves on the ground that we had not observed the armistice, and had killed a vast number of their people. The fact is that, the very day on which they showed the decree ordering protection for the Ministers, they fired on us in the evening, and through the night they were seen preparing for a general assault, which our people averted by a successful sortie.

For a few days there was a slight relaxation in the vigour of attack, and something like incipient intercourse began to show itself. Soldiers in the opposing ranks approached and conversed with each other. A young Frenchman, who had been captured, was well treated by the enemy, and, what he much appreciated, well fed. A deserter from our ranks was, along with the young Frenchman, returned to us with compliments.

The ground of these courtesies we now know to have been the alarm created by the capture of Tien Tsin. Immediately after that event, which occurred on the 14th of July, Li Hung Chang was appointed Plenipotentiary to negotiate by cable for a cessation of hostilities. That meant an effort to stop the advance on Peking.

It was during this time that the good offices of our Government,

A Chinese view of the murder of the Japanese chancelier, regarded by them as an execution, in the presence of Chinese troops and Boxers

as well as those of the Courts of Europe and Japan, were solicited by China. The Secretary of State replied by demanding a communication from Minister Conger as a condition indispensable to compliance with that request. Our Minister was accordingly permitted to send a despatch in cipher, which, so far from tending to stop the advance of the army of relief, set forth our extreme peril, and had a mighty influence in quickening their movements.

Toward the end of the siege the daily and nightly attacks upon us were renewed with increasing fury—doubtless because their efforts to stop the advance had proved abortive.

The deserter above referred to was a Norwegian missionary, Nestigard. His mind had never been well balanced, and he is the man of whom we have spoken as going stark mad. Placed under surveillance he resented restraint, and in the night made his escape. In a searching examination at the head-quarters of Yung Lu, he no doubt revealed all he knew about our situation: the small number of ponies we had left, the diminution of our other stores, and the imperfection of our means of defence. He confessed to having told the enemy that the reason why they killed so few within our enclosure was because they aimed too high. It was the general opinion that the wretch ought to be shot. Sir Claude MacDonald, however, spared him on account of his insanity, and from that day it took the time of seven men to guard him!

During the first stage of the siege I noticed a handsome young lady, one of the guests from abroad, sitting for her portrait, while a lady artist, Miss Payen, with untrembling hand, transferred her pleasing features to canvas. I wondered at the composure of both. Nor was my astonishment diminished when, in the evening, I overheard that same young lady saying to Captain Myers:

"Now, remember, should they overpower us, your first duty will be to shoot me."

Another lady, the mother of a family, displayed equal nerve. Her husband had given her a revolver with the injunction, in the case supposed, first to shoot her daughters, and then to shoot herself, if he should not be at hand to relieve her of that painful duty. Both he and she are good Christians, and it is believed that similar arrangements were made in the case of every woman within the legation. In our circumstances there was no time for casuistry.

How soon our protecting wall might fall a heap of ruins no one could tell; but sure we were that the enemy were undermining it night and day. Whether the countermining operations would prove successful was far from certain. The Chinese are peculiarly skilful in this mode of attack. They had tried it successfully on the French legation, which was almost demolished. When two buildings of that legation were blown into the air, a sentry on the roof of one of them, who went up along with the ruins, came down Unhurt! To his surprise, he found himself alive and buried to the chin in the midst of *débris*.

Though we tried to look cheerful and to feel hopeful, yet when disappointed in our expectation of speedy relief, we were led to fear the worst, we said, "God's will be done. If we perish our blood will be the regeneration of China. As our Lord shed his for the world, it is a small thing for us to shed ours for China."

What wonder that in those dark hours we were reported as slain and the final scene depicted in shocking detail, our likenesses were placed on the pages of Magazines, in the sable hues of mourning accompanied by our obituaries. It is not always a disadvantage to know what our friends think of us. If the reader will turn to the appendix he may there see an obituary of Sir R. Hart, which shows what his friends think of him.

Almost from the beginning, we had sought to keep up our courage by the use of Scripture texts. They were usually supplied by Mrs. Arthur Smith, and I posted them at the gate-house, hoping they might catch the eye of some who had little time for Scripture reading. One day she handed me a text which she said was selected for her by Mrs. Conger, who met with it in her daily reading. We were all struck with its adaptation to the circumstances in which we were then placed. It was as follows:

> *We would not, brethren, have you ignorant of our trouble which came to us in Asia, that we were pressed out of measure, above strength, insomuch that we despaired even of life; but we had the sentence of death in ourselves, that we should not trust in ourselves, but in God which raiseth the dead; who delivered us from so great a death, and doth deliver. In whom we trust that he will yet deliver us. Ye also helping together by prayer for us, that for the gift bestowed upon us by the means of many persons thanks may be given by many on our behalf.—2 Cor. 1:8-11.*

Whenever I had occasion to leave the gate during those long summer days I usually requested Dr. Arthur Smith to take my place as Inspector of Passes. He always spent much time sitting by my side, attracted not so much by the charms of my conversation as by the opportunity which that post afforded for observing the life and manners of many nationalities. *His* conversation I greatly enjoyed, and I found that even the gravity of our situation failed to repress his flow of genial humour. A search of family records would probably confirm our suspicion that one of his ancestors was named Sidney.

Pointing to Professor Gamewell, as he sped to and fro on his bicycle inspecting our defence works, he exclaimed:

That man seems to be a limited omnipresence.

I cite the expression not so much for its novelty as its truth. Gamewell had displayed his skill in the art of fortification before the missionaries took refuge in the legation. The several Protestant missions had joined their forces at the extensive grounds of the Methodist Mission, and, supplied with a reinforcement of twenty marines under the command of Captain Hall; they resolved to maintain the position.

On the death of Baron Ketteler, to their great disappointment, Captain Hall suddenly gave the order for its evacuation.

The committees which they had there formed for defence and supply, and especially the experience acquired, came into play at the British legation, where Sir Claude MacDonald welcomed them with as much cordiality as he had accorded to the people of the legations.

The native Christians were, as we have said, also welcomed, sheltered, and defended, though not within the same enclosure. When the question had come up in regard to them some days previously in a council of the Ministers, some members of the diplomatic corps objected to receiving so large a body of natives on account of the danger of running short of provisions. The missionaries, however, had resolved to live or die with their converts, and their noble devotion was fully appreciated by the American and British Ministers, as well as by the greater part of the diplomatic body.

Here is a letter in which the American Minister; gracefully acknowledges the share which they and the missionaries bore in the work of defence:

LEGATION OF THE UNITED STATES OF AMERICA, PEKING, CHINA,
AUGUST 18, 1900.

To the Besieged American Missionaries:
To one and all of you, so providentially saved from threatened

massacre, I beg, in this hour of our deliverance, to express what I know to be the universal sentiments of the Diplomatic Corps, the sincere appreciation of, and professed profound gratitude for the inestimable help which you and the native Christians under your charge have rendered toward our preservation.

Without your intelligent and successful planning and the un-complaining execution of the Chinese, I believe our salvation would have been impossible.

By your courteous consideration of me, and your continued patience under most trying occasions, I have been deeply touched, and for it all I thank you most heartily.

I hope and believe somehow, in God's unerring plan, your sac-rifices and dangers will bear rich fruit in the material and spir-itual welfare of the people to whom you have so nobly devoted your lives and work.

Assuring you of my personal respect and gratitude, believe me,

Very sincerely yours,

(Signed)   E. H. Conger.

We heard with much satisfaction that Li Hung Chang had been appointed to negotiate peace. A lover of his country, whatever else he may be, he has the further merit of being loyal to the reigning dynasty. Unlike the Dowager, he has always shown himself an enlightened friend of progress. No statesman of China, not even that southern viceroy whose famous book points out that education is the "only hope of China," can contest with him the palm of being pre-emi-nently the patron of the New Education. Some years ago I published a paper in a Chinese magazine pointing out his achievements in this direction. He was greatly pleased, as I was informed by his private secretary, and without hesitation contributed a laudatory preface to a book which I had prepared on *Christian Psychology*.

He had written similar prefaces for several scientific works pre-pared by me in former years. His reading of those works may not have disposed him to recommend to the young Emperor the creation of a university in the capital, but it did induce him to recommend their author for the presidency of that institution. When he proposed to me to accept the position, I consented to undertake it for two or three years, alleging my age as a reason for not thinking of a longer term of service.

Surveying me from head to foot, "I guess," said he, "you're good

LI HUNG CHANG CHINA'S GREATEST STATESMAN
AND PEACE COMMISSIONER.

for another ten years: I wish I had your legs." (He is partially paralyzed in his lower limbs.)

"It is this that counts with a statesman," said I, tapping on my forehead.

"Ah," he replied, with a smile, "but you are good at both ends."

The first place I visited after returning to the United States legation was the new university. I found it occupied for a barrack by Russian troops. On going into my house, a handsome building in Mandarin style newly erected for the use of the president, I found that soldiers (not Russian) or Boxers had smashed every article of furniture, and dumped all my books, as well as those of the university, including valuable collections of Chinese authors, into the wells and cisterns. What wonder when they had trodden under foot, or burnt to ashes, the magnificent library of the Hanlin Academy! My books they subjected to immersion rather than conflagration, because the building, having been a princely palace, they were forbidden to destroy by fire.

The wires of a piano and the lungs of a melodeon lay scattered about the floor, and on every side were to be seen fragments of Broken China.

The telegraph informs us that the Russians, in whose bank they are deposited, have announced their intention to confiscate the funds of the university. After paying off our professors, on my requisition, they declined to go on paying indefinitely—and declared to me their purpose to hold the funds in payment of Russian claims. Will Li Hung Chang, its founder and patron, consent to an act of spoliation so opposed to the usages of civilized nations!

No man is more sensible to the estimate in which he is held in Western countries. Four years ago I called on him, along with the Rev, Gilbert Reid, to solicit a letter of recommendation for an educational enterprise (the International Institute) which Mr. Reid had taken in hand.

"Why!" said Li Hung Chang, "has not the Yamen already given him a letter of recommendation?" (It had been done at Li's instance.)

"True," said I; "but the Western world don't know anything about the Tsung Li Yamen."

"What!" exclaimed Li. "Don't they know that we have a *waipu*—a foreign office?"

"Yes," said I, "but there are only two names in all China that they know anything about—one is Confucius, the other is Li Hung Chang."

Pei Tang: the French Cathedral held by Roman Catholics until relieved by Japanese.

He smiled from ear to ear, and said, "I'll give it," immediately writing a most flattering testimonial.

CHAPTER 7

Rescue and Retribution

We had feared, not without reason, that the Chinese forces which had gone out to meet the army of relief might, on being vanquished, retreat to the city, reinforce our assailants, and destroy us all before succour could arrive. This they took care not to do, after their experience of European arms; yet certain it is that our besiegers renewed their attacks with increasing fury as our friends approached the wall. General Tung Fu Siang even promised the Dowager to wipe us out in five days. The attack on the night of the 13th of August was unusually terrific, and we looked forward with no little apprehension to what might happen on the following night. Happily, before the following night the rescue was effected, and our enemies dispersed. Said General Chaffee to me:

> It is lucky that we arrived one day ahead of time. The leaders had agreed to attack the city on the 15th, but the Russians, from whatever motive, having stolen a march on us, it was impossible for the rest of us to be left behind, and so we all pressed forward to be ready to make the assault on the 14th. As we were bivouacked near the city on the night of the 13th, I heard the roar of Chinese guns playing on the legation, and I said, 'I fear we are already too late.' I could not sleep for anxiety.

The Russians were no doubt animated by the same feeling, and thus providentially the enemy had no opportunity to renew their attack.

I felt proud of my country when I learned how our Republic had stretched out her mighty arms to protect her citizens beyond the sea; and how promptly our President had assumed the responsibility of action. And how proud I felt of our countrymen when I heard the story of their valour as exhibited in the march from the sea!

On the 17th of June the admirals demanded the surrender of the forts, in their ignorance professing only to desire to aid the government against the Boxers. The American admiral, I regret to say, declined to join in the demand or to participate in the assault. By what means he and our commanders were brought to change their views, I know not; but in the subsequent operations Americans have no reason to be ashamed of their record.

In 1858 I had seen those forts silenced and captured in twenty minutes. In 1859 I had witnessed the defeat of a combined squadron of thirteen English and French gun-boats by those same forts, nor was I without fear that on this occasion, strengthened as they had been by all the arts of modern warfare, they might have proved too strong for the attacking force. History might, indeed, have had to chronicle another defeat but for an unforeseen circumstance. The Chinese gunners had trained their heavy artillery on the gun-boats, but, swinging with the tide, they all shifted their position except one. That one alone was struck when the firing commenced.

The return fire from the gun-boats soon silenced the batteries, and the Chinese artillerymen took to flight. In their haste they forgot to break down a drawbridge; a storming party succeeded in passing over without opposition, and the flags of the Allies were soon floating on their ramparts.

The advance to Tien Tsin was stoutly opposed; the Chinese in many instances fighting with great bravery. Three times at least was the American contingent repulsed, but, undismayed, their brave officers led them on, and they contributed no small share to the relief of the beleaguered settlement. In those battles Colonel Liscum lost his life, and not a few of his men fell with him.

For ten days the foreign settlement had been closely pressed by the enemy; square miles of native houses were reduced to ashes; the Hongs of foreign merchants were battered down, and their palatial residences were left in ruins. The women and children of the community were huddled together in the basement of Gordon Hall to get shelter from the bomb-shells, and the upper stories of that fine edifice threatened every moment to come down upon their heads.

On the 23rd their deliverers appeared on the opposite bank of the river (the Russians first), and they were saved. It was not, however, until three weeks later that the Allies were able to force their way into the citadel of the native town.

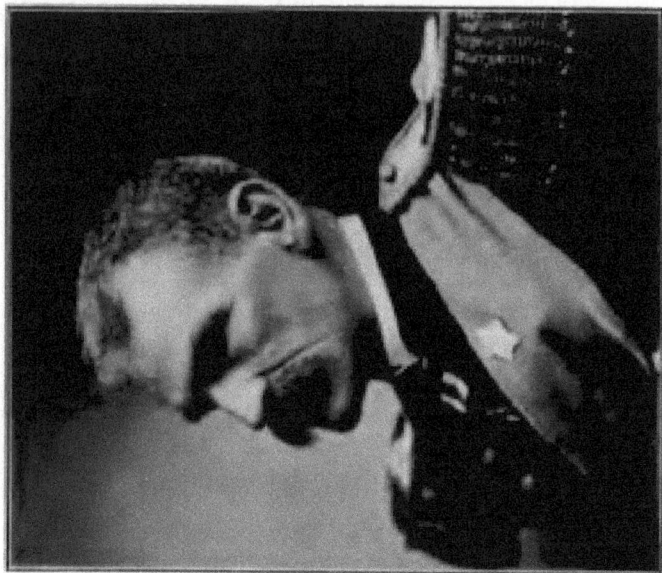

General Chaffee

Colonel Liscum

The next step was to move on the capital, distant eighty miles. The combined forces selected for that expedition did not much exceed 15,000 men—a strong detachment having been left behind for the protection of Tien Tsin. Their march was not begun until the 1st of August, and it is said that, owing to the heat and the rainy season, some of the commanders were in favour of postponing the advance until September. But General Gaselee, in command of the British forces, and General Chaffee, in command of the American forces, supported by the Japanese, insisted on going forward without delay. The question was decided by the bold declaration of General Gaselee that should all others refuse to proceed he, with the British contingent, would at once push on to Peking. But for this prompt action their work would have been that of vengeance, not rescue.

At two or three points on the way they encountered even fiercer opposition than before; but, cutting their way through overwhelming bodies of native troops, they pressed steadily forward.

We had some intimation of the commencement of their march, but of their progress we heard nothing; and, as day succeeded day during that tedious fortnight, we speculated much on the composition of the force, and the disposition of its leaders, and we feared that political jealousies, rather than the prowess of the enemy, had held them in check. We suspected that General Mismanagement was responsible for this delay; and someone suggested that, whoever led the divisions, the whole movement must be under the command of General Slowcome.

The resistance offered by the garrison on the outer walls was not of long duration. The fate of the capital was decided by the fall of Tien Tsin, and the battles at intermediate points inspired the Government and its armies with the utmost terror. After a short struggle, the soldiers who held the walls fled in confusion, and our troops entered in triumph.

The Empress Dowager and her Court made their escape from the Western gates almost at the moment when our deliverers were battering down the Eastern gates. More than half the population abandoned their dwellings, and fled from the city. In their haste, they left behind them wardrobes filled with costly furs, their floors were strewn with the richest silks; and in some cases the whole ground was covered with nuggets of silver. What a temptation to plunder! The punishment of the guilty city would not have been too severe had it been formally given up to be sacked by the soldiery. It was not formally given up to pillage, but the commanders, though announcing their intention to forbid looting, appeared to be in no hurry to impose a check on the mingled wrath and cupidity of their men.

The old practice is dear to the hearts of the soldiery. There is no nation whose soldiers have not taken part in it; whether from a feeling that in so doing they are wreaking well-merited vengeance on the Chinese people, or whether because fruit is the more attractive in consequence of being forbidden, it is hard to say. At all events, the expected prohibition was long delayed, giving many of them time to fill their pockets and their knapsacks. I even heard of a soldier who had loaded a wheelbarrow with nuggets of silver. Having his attention called by a comrade to some pieces that were spilled over by the jolting of the vehicle, he laughed and said, "No matter, you take care of them."

He was, in fact, impatient to convey his booty to a place of safety. A secure place for it was not easy to find; as all were apprehensive that they would be called on to surrender it, they did their utmost to get rid of it as soon as possible, hence the immense amount of bullion offered for sale in little driblets by individual soldiers, who appeared to be straggling here and there in quest of something. That something was not more booty, but a purchaser for what they had. It was impossible to pass through the street in the vicinity of the Great Front Gate without encountering soldiers of various nationalities who, making signs to the passer-by, stealthily drew from their sleeves or pockets silver, gems, small works of art, and curios of all descriptions, which were not too large to be concealed about the person.

In this matter, as in others, there is a wide difference to be observed in the degree of restraint imposed by the several countries. Some of them allow their soldiers practically unlimited license, others, notably the British Generals, forbid all private embezzlement, and collect, as far as possible, every sort of plunder into a common stock to be sold at auction for the common benefit. Hence it was that for weeks caravans of mules and donkeys, and oftentimes long trains of wagons, all under the British or Japanese flags, might be seen wending their way to the headquarters of one or other of those nations, laden with abandoned treasure, silks, furs, and grain.

Of the public treasures, the Japanese, knowing the exact points to seize on, succeeded in getting the lion's share. As to private property, much of it was abandoned, without a policeman, a domestic, or even a dog for its protection, so that it was wholly at the mercy of the first-comer. What wonder, then, that for several days the soldiers of all nationalities repaid themselves for hardship and danger by rioting in the midst of booty.

Well were it had they confined themselves to the looting of empty houses. Some of them, I blush to say, violated the sacredness of the homes of poor families who had been unable to make their escape. The greatest number of outrages of this description were charged on a battalion of Chinese soldiery from Wei Hai Wei, who fought under the British flag, and were led by British officers. Though they have learned British discipline, they have not acquired British morals.

The missionaries and their converts, emancipated from duress but without a house of their own to which they could return, were permitted by the military authorities to find quarters for themselves in any of the abandoned houses they might choose to occupy. With this wide range of selection, some installed themselves, with their flocks, in the mansions of princes; others occupied the houses of lesser nobility, or wealthy mandarins. Nor were those authorities slow to exercise a similar liberty on their own account. Places more august and sacred than princes' mansions were seized for their own use and that of their soldiers. General Gaselee pitched his camp within the holy grounds (the *temenos*) of the temple of Heaven, and made his headquarters in the Emperor's carriage park. The Americans took possession of the Temple of Agriculture, where the Emperor prays in person for a good harvest.

In a commodious but not imposing building, I passed a few days under the hospitable care of the ladies of the Presbyterian Mission. While there, the missionaries having gone out, I was called by my servants to see a foreigner who had come in without sending his card. I found him making his exit from the apartments of the Rev. J. L. Whiting, with Mr. Whiting's rifle in one hand and his revolver in the other. He was, I am sorry to say, a white man, and, laying down the weapons on my demand, he confessed himself an American!

The missionaries being in great anxiety as to a food-supply for their converts, accompanied by Rev. Dr. Wherry and Rev. J. L. Whiting, I proceeded to do a little looting on their behalf.

I had heard of a deserted grain-shop in the inner city, close to the university. There we discovered a considerable store of wheat, millet, and other grain. Loading it in carts, we carried away not less than two hundred bushels. Calling aloud to the proprietor, I informed him that on the presentation of his bill I would pay the full value of his property, but echo was the only answer that returned.

The Rev. E. G. Tewkesbury, who, during the siege had been Chief of Commissariat, now showed that he knew well how to obtain supplies for his needy Christians. The American Board Mission being installed in a prince's mansion, he discovered there and in neighbouring buildings large quantities of furs, silks, and other valuables, which, having previously advertised them to the army and the legations, he sold at public auction for the benefit of native converts. Of those things, Mr. Squiers, the gallant Secretary of the United States legation, became a large purchaser, and the Rev. W. B. Stelle, a self-supporting missionary, who, before the siege, had along with Dr. Ament made a notable excursion through regions infested by Boxers, and who during the siege had done yeoman's duty in bearing arms, now purchased four boxes of furs to be sold in New York for the benefit of suffering Christians. So much for the charges of looting that have been brought against missionaries!

Gladly do I share in the blame which they incur, and confess myself equally guilty with them, though the only object which I appropriated to my own use was a goat-skin rug. This I found on the floor of a nice house which my servants chose for me just at the west side of the Great Front Gate. That building I occupied alone for a few days, and whenever I went out it was sure to be invaded by straggling soldiers of various nationalities—Hindoo, Russian, or American—who carried away some things; and, as my servants said, threatened to split open my trunks to get at their contents, suspecting that they were full of loot. So frequently did this occur that I felt compelled to seek an abode along with others, where we could have the benefits of mutual protection.

The great metropolis was subdivided between the various divisions of the conquering force. The northern half of the Tartar City was occupied by the Japanese; the central portion, together with a part of the inner, or Imperial, city by the Russians, who erected batteries on the beautiful hill within the Imperial Gardens, and seized our new university for barracks.

The portions which fell to the lot of the other six nations it is unnecessary to point out. All those divisions were signalized as under the control of some foreign power by the display on all public buildings of one or other of their Eight Banners.

The Eight Banners of the Manchus were nowhere to be seen, but, in their stead, floated from innumerable private dwellings small copies of those foreign flags, inscribed with Chinese letters, indicating that their occupants "were faithful subjects of the Great Sunrise Empire"; or, "Submissive to the sway of the Russian *Czar*"; or, "Humble subjects of the great United States," etc.

On some of them might be read an inscription in "pidgin" English, or bad French:

We be good people—no makee bobbery! Please, don't shoot.

So effectually cowed were these lately belligerent multitudes that, had they been required to worship the Crucifix and submit to Christian baptism, they would have shown no hesitation in doing so. The proud city, the Babylon of the East, is brought down to the dust. Her gate-towers have been burned: some by her own people, others by the conquering army; of her public buildings some have been destroyed by the foreign legions; but destruction on a larger scale in every quarter has been perpetrated by the mad fury of the Boxers. It will take half a century to restore its former splendour.

Yet did the Allies, in the midst of this devastation, purposely spare the Imperial palaces. In 1860 the Anglo-French expedition destroyed the summer-palace, as a punishment for an outrage on a flag of truce. Would not the Allies on this occasion have been fully justified in blowing up the palace of the Empress Dowager, as a punishment for her perfidy and cruelty? They chose, instead, merely to make a triumphal march into the *penetralia* of the Forbidden City, in order to impress the Chinese Court with a sense of humiliation, and convince the Chinese people of the victory of the foreign forces. They hope that the Emperor and his Court may be induced to return to that magnificent abode. May they not be mistaken in this expectation? For is it not well known that there are certain birds which, when you so much as touch the interior of their nest, never, under any circumstances, return to occupy it again?

Pao Ting Fu, the capital of the province, as the scene of unheard-of atrocities, has been occupied by a joint expedition of British, German, and French; its walls broken down, some of its public buildings destroyed, and some of its highest officials condemned to death. The city has been intentionally subjected to disgrace. It deserves to be sown with salt.

Tai Yuen, the capital of the neighbouring Province of Shansi, deserves a similar fate, for there it was that the truculent Governor, Yu Hien, imbrued his hands in the blood of over fifty missionaries. Nine-

THE CENTRAL MOAT OR CANAL IN THE FORBIDDEN CITY

ty-three in all, Catholic and Protestant, are reported as having perished in this tempest of fire and blood. The details of their sufferings will not bear repetition, yet we may say of them, as an English poet says of the victims of the *Sepoy* Mutiny, that:

Every outraged woman died a virgin undefiled,
And every hewn-up infant was a Bethlehem's holy child.

If few foreigners outside of the missionary circle lost their lives, it was because there were few, or none, exposed to the savage foe in unprotected places. Little cared that savage foe whether they wreaked their vengeance on church or railway. Anything foreign was to them like a red rag to an infuriated bull. In one of their manifestoes they ended by saying: "When we have slaughtered them all, we shall tear up the railways, cut down the telegraphs, and then finish off by burning their steamboats."

CHAPTER 8

Reconstruction

The telegraph informs us that the representatives of the great powers in China are substantially agreed as to the demands they are to make upon the Chinese Government. It remains to be seen whether a government exists capable of complying with those demands, or willing to do so. That the Court will never consent to the humiliation of returning to Peking, to lay its neck beneath the headsman's axe, is highly probable. Nor is it unlikely that it will prove itself utterly unable to sustain the debt which it must incur to indemnify eight foreign nations for a long campaign, and their people, together with a large body of native Christians for the destruction of their property.

The war must go on until the Manchu Government consents to do this, and to give suitable guarantees against the recurrence of any similar uprising in the future. They must be disarmed, and rendered incapable of again jeopardizing the peace of the civilized world. The tiger's teeth must be drawn, his claws cut short by the destruction of his arsenals, and a prohibition be placed on the importation of munitions of war. Let China be compelled to march in the van of those nations of whom it is said, *they shall learn war no more.*

It is related of a Methodist preacher that a notorious bully swore that the next time he came around he would put a stop to his psalm-singing and his exhortations. He, however, reckoned without his host, for the preacher was himself a Boxer, and, when attacked, succeeded in less than no time in flooring his antagonist. Jumping astride of him, he pounded away until the bystanders begged him to let the poor devil up.

"No," said he, "I will not let the devil up. My object is to keep the devil down; nor will I cease pounding until this wretched man promises to seek the salvation of his soul."

This is what I would have the Allies do in the case of China. I would have no state church established in any portion of that empire; but our worst enemy in the last resort is heathen darkness, and, if we would not let the "devil up" to attack us again, we must wage war on the powers of darkness until the true light shall be allowed to shine without hindrance into every nook and corner of the land.

There must be no abridgment of the rights and privileges of missionaries; no relaxation in the efforts of the home churches. The wondrous awakening, comparable to a shaking among the dry bones, which took place during the short interval preceding the Dowager's unlucky *coup d'état* is sure to be succeeded by a national resurrection on a much broader scale. We may justly look for *novus ordo seclorum*, to begin with the twentieth century. Let America, as she has so nobly borne her part in the rescue of the legations, bear her full share in the Christian crusade of the coming age.

American interests of all kinds are striking, their roots deep into the soil of China. Among the railways radiating from Hankow, that great centre of population, wealth, and power, no line will exceed in importance that which an American Company has laid out through Hunan, Kwangsi, and Kwangtung to the seaport of Canton. To such enterprises increased value is given by the resolution of the powers to maintain, if possible, the integrity of the empire. The open door appears to be their settled policy. Let the door be forever open to light as well as to trade. We are informed that, of all the higher institutions established in late years for the education of the people of China, there is not one that has not had an American citizen at its head. Let the number of such be multiplied, and not diminished, in years to come.

The representatives of the powers agree, we are told, in proposing to recall the Emperor. So natural is this idea that no one can claim originality for having hit upon it, yet the present writer was perhaps the first to propose it as the basis for a scheme of reconstruction.

My views on the subject were reduced to writing as early as the middle of June, and put in print shortly after the raising of the siege. They are here copied from the Peking and Tien Tsin *Times* of September 15, 1900:

THE PROBLEM OF RECONSTRUCTION
BY DR. W. A. P. MARTIN, OF PEKING

It may, perhaps, add somewhat to the interest of the following paragraphs to know that they were written at the beginning of the siege, and at that time placed in the hands of some of the diplomats in the capital. Now, after the flight of the Dowager and Court, I find in them nothing to alter or modify, and, to make this apparent, I reproduce the original with quotation marks:

'The question of the hour is how to restore order, and at the same time secure the fruits of a revolution which has so unexpectedly placed the fate of China in the hands of foreign Powers, Four measures appear to cover the ground:

'1. To undo the mischief done by her, let the Empress Dowager be sent into exile, and let the Emperor be restored to his proper authority, subject to a concert of the great Powers.

'2. Let all the acts of the Empress Dowager, beginning with her *coup d'état* and including the appointment of her partisans, be cancelled, except such as are approved by the new administration.

'3. Let the Emperor's programme of reform be resumed, and carried out with the sanction of the Powers.

'4. Let the Powers mark out their spheres of interest, and each appoint a representative to control the action of provincial governments within its own sphere.

'For China, complete independence is neither possible nor advisable. The above plan would keep existing machinery in operation, avert anarchy, favour progress, and conciliate the support of the most enlightened among the Chinese people. The alternative is the overthrow of the present dynasty and the formal partition of the empire—a process involving long and bitter conflicts. By the scheme proposed, foreign Powers will have time to mature their policy, and to introduce gradual reforms, gaining vastly more than they could hope to secure by open or violent absorption. It is easy to govern China through the Chinese; impossible otherwise.

'Peking, June 18, 1900.'

In looking over these paragraphs the only thing I have to add (and that only by way of explanation) is a suggestion that the joint commission of foreign Powers should have an absolute veto on all measures hostile to their common interests. Besides this, they should have the initiation, though not exclusive, in progressive reforms.   W. A. P. M.

Tien Tsin, September 13, 1900.

This brief outline I may amplify and explain, but even at this date (November 6) I would not alter it in any essential particular.

It requires, however, a little explanation to guard against misapprehension.

As to the first point, at this date, all parties appear to see eye to eye; and the restoration of the Emperor will be a *fait accompli* if not opposed by the Empress Dowager. As to the second, it is not intended to suggest any direct penalty. Deprivation of power is in itself sufficient punishment for a woman of her proud and haughty disposition. That she merits to be treated with greater severity, no one will question; but many considerations militate against meting out to her an extreme measure of justice. The Southern Viceroys have been fairly faithful to their engagements to restrain the people of their Provinces from any sort of outbreak, either directed against foreigners or native Christians. They have succeeded in fact in checking the spread of the Boxer fanaticism within their boundaries.

When, therefore, such men plead for indulgent treatment toward the Empress Dowager, they have a right to be heard. In begging for "indulgent treatment," they by no means demand the restoration of her power; merely the preservation of that which the Chinese consider as above power and above life itself, that mysterious something which they call "face." On this point they would no doubt be fully satisfied to see her sent into retirement at some point within the Empire, say Jehol in Mongolia, or Sianfu in Shensi, which she has now chosen for the seat of her court.

Should the Emperor return to Peking, the Dowager ought by all means not to be allowed to accompany him. In fact, the wider distance by which they are separated, the better; and as she has of late shown herself an avowed patroness of the enemies of railways and telegraphs, there should be neither one nor the other between her and her Imperial Nephew. Should she merely be sent into retirement at her old palace on the Kwen Ming Lake (near Peking), she would inevitably continue to be as she was in her previous retirement, a power behind the throne, handling the cards with a dexterity acquired from forty years of manipulation. Were the powers to insist on banishing her to some Elba, beyond the boundaries of her own country, the loyal Viceroys, who have succeeded so admirably in steering a middle course between their duty to her and their obligations to foreign countries, would undoubtedly regard that penalty as a national indignity.

The fourth raises the most serious question which the powers have to deal with. It is one which might easily set them at loggerheads, and plunge China into the vortex of a sanguinary conflict, a war of giants in comparison with which the struggles of native princes are like the battles of pigmies and cranes. Nor is it now raised for the first time. It originated more than a score of years ago.—Each of China's neighbours, especially Great Britain, France, and Russia, having at that early date fixed their eyes, and also planted their feet on a portion of the Empire which they intended to claim as their special sphere, or in the event of a break-up, as their territorial dependency. Since the war with Japan, two other claimants have come forward, the Sunrise Empire and Germany; and Chinese statesmen were three years ago wrought up to a high pitch of excitement by having placed before their eyes a new map of China with the red lines of division, marking out her territory as partitioned amongst the great powers of Europe and the East.

Now, after this tremendous upheaval, the question of partition or delimitation of spheres of influence looms up like a spectre. The central regions of those spheres are sufficiently understood; Russia has hers in the North and North-east; France, her ally, having hers in the South and Southwest; Great Britain having chosen hers in the centre, the magnificent and well watered valley of the Yangtse, which rivals in extent and wealth of productions our own Mississippi Valley. For Japan, as she has already got Formosa, it is natural that she should demand a foothold on the opposite coast. Germany, having planted herself already on the coast, is reaching westward to the far interior, and it remains to be seen how much of the *hinterland* will be allowed to go with her seaport under the name of "sphere of influence."

Let us take another glance at these indefinite claims with a view to ascertaining somewhat more exactly their probable extent.

With regard to that of Russia. Never since Yermak, with his *Cossacks*, crossed the Ural Mountains, and annexed Siberia, three hundred years ago, has she made such a sweeping annexation of territory as she now proposes to effect under the veil of a sphere of influence. Her sphere will unquestionably comprehend the three great Provinces of the Northeast, which form Manchuria, the original home of the reigning dynasty. To this she will add the whole of Mongolia, Turkestan, Ili, and the Pamirs to the North of India.

Already has she cast covetous eyes on the entire belt of Northern Provinces, which border on the Great Wall. There can, however, be no doubt that the other powers will combine to oppose the acquisition by her of any exclusive preponderance in that region. This, more than anything else, I take to be the meaning of that remarkable Fourth Clause in the recent agreement between England and Germany. That belt of Provinces if withheld from the predominant influence of any one power, will therefore remain as the nucleus of an Empire, a common ground for the combined influence of all.

The basis for the gradual absorption of Chinese territory was laid by Russia as early as 1858, when the four powers, England, France, Russia, and the United States were negotiating their treaties at Tien Tsin. Two of them were belligerents, each with the right to carve out for itself with its own sword as much territory as its ally would consent to. The others possessed also some advantage in being neutrals, and skilfully did Russia play her cards, for she obtained, as the price of neutrality on that occasion, the cession of a strip of sea-coast 700 miles in length, extending southward from the mouth of the Amoor, and confronting the Empire of Japan. One day, during the negotiations, Pien Lao Ye, one of the Secretaries of Queileang, came to me to beg me (I was then interpreter) to persuade Mr. Reed, the American Minister, to use his influence with the Russian Minister, to induce him to withdraw his demand for that portion of Manchuria. Said Pien,

"With us, it is not a question of territory, but of the inhabitants. The Emperor has such a vast domain that he would scarcely miss a small strip like that, but within that small strip are 7,000 Manchu families. Them he regards as his near kinsmen, or rather as his own children, and he cannot bear to turn them over to the sway of a foreign power."

It was pathetic, his affection (like that of Mrs. Jellaby) for those far-off tribes; but needless to say, the American Minister saw no reason for interposing to check the advance of Russia. In addition to the Valley of the Yangtse, Great Britain will either stretch her shield over the whole course of the Pearl River, east and west, including the Great mart of Canton; or that region, the original seat of foreign trade in China, might, like the Northern Provinces, be reserved as common ground.

Germany is already planning a railway to the capital of Shan Tung. In her newspapers she speaks of the province as German China, nor is it improbable that her claims upon the *hinterland* may be made to cover the South of Chili and the North of Honan, both bounded by the Yellow River.

The Province of Fo Kien will be regarded by Japan as her appropriate sphere, especially as she as compelled by the Powers to forego the occupation of Liao Tung, or Southern Manchuria. It was a master stroke on the part of Russia, thus to oust a victorious nation and reserve for herself a rich region which that Power already held by right of conquest.

Two years ago Germany proposed the appointment, at the provincial capital, of a German Governor to sit beside the representative of Chinese majesty. The scheme was not carried out, nor do I, in suggesting the appointment within each sphere of a high functionary to "control "the action of provincial governors, intend that they shall themselves be Governors. The word "control" I employ rather in the French sense as indicating their office to take note of and restrain, if necessary, the action of the native governors. Such powers would not be difficult to define. Indeed, had there been present in Tsinanfu a German official (*comptroller* we may call him) alongside of Yu Hien to play the spy on his movements, and impose a check on his extravagance, we never should have heard of his distributing arms to the Boxers; and this great revolution would have been nipped in the bud.

Austria and Italy will each claim something to be called a sphere. For Austria, perhaps, it may be the Island of Chusan; for Italy some part of the adjacent mainland, where she has tried in vain to set her foot.

As for the United States: We carefully abstained from demanding territory as the price of our neutrality, forty years ago. In the recent conflict, I am proud to say, *we have not been neutral*; yet are we less disposed than any other nation to indulge in territorial aggrandizement? Perhaps because we have enough on our hands at home and abroad. If I were to point out any place within the bounds of China where, in lieu of the payment of war expenses, China might concede us a *pied à terre*, it would be the island of Hainan, a stepping-stone between Hong-Kong and the Philippines. It is half as large as Sicily, and capable of being made equally rich in its productions.

We should then have a *tangible ground* for demanding to be heard on all great questions relating to the future of China.

It was not land-grabbing which impelled Great Britain sixty years ago to demand the island of Hong-Kong. What she wanted was a *Pousto*, a fulcrum from which to move the world; nor for us will it be unduly aggressive to negotiate for the island of Hainan.

With what is called by the opprobrious name of Imperialism, I have little sympathy, but natural expansion or growth is quite a different thing. For America, no more than for Great Britain, will it do

Her proud pre-eminence to abdicate,
Through craven fear of growing great.

It was not Imperialism that led the Russian Empire to overstep the Urals, and make her way to the Pacific. What lover of his race would wish the centuries rolled back because she encountered a few Turgouths, Buriats, and Samoyedes in her pathway? Had she from want of energy neglected her opportunity, instead of that vast domain containing the longest railway in the world, the North of Asia would have presented only a battle-ground for savage tribes. Had our fore-fathers neglected their opportunities, we should not today have possessed a foot of land to the west of the Mississippi; nor would Florida have been one among the Stars upon our flag.

It is by natural growth that we have expanded our territory to the Pacific, and extended our influence to Japan and China. It was by the embracing of an offered opportunity by our statesmen that Japan was lifted out of her old groove, and set going on her new career. In that empire, so conspicuous has our influence been, that the language we speak is described as *Americano* (not English). In China, up to the present time, our political influence has been inconspicuous; but now a great opportunity presents itself, and God forbid that it should pass unimproved. In my view, no great extent of territory is required to give us the needed foothold. If an island be not desirable, a sea-port on the mainland will give us all that is needed, namely: a shelter for our naval squadrons; a post where our armies may rendezvous in case they are required either to oppose the absorption of China by some grasping nationality, or to quell another uprising against the civilized world such as we are now witnessing.

This is demanded by our natural growth. Without it our growing commerce and our magnificent railway and mining enterprises in the interior would be insecure.

With regard to the final settlement, English organs in China hold substantially the foregoing views. As to what the Germans think on the subject, we may gather from the *Ostasiatische Lloyd*, the German organ in the Far East. An extract, under twelve heads, in the *North China Herald* of October 3, 1900, reads as follows:

1. No withdrawal from Peking until the whole matter is settled.

2. No Chinese connected with the recent outrages to be accepted as negotiators, and the negotiations on the side of the allies to be conducted by one representative, say the Commander-in-Chief.

3. The instigators of outrages and others to be punished in their purse, their most sensitive part.

4. H. M. Kuang Hsu to be restored, if possible; if not, a new Emperor not connected with the Empress Dowager's clique. Prince Tuan's son to be deposed from the position of Heir Apparent. The Empress Dowager to be allowed to retire into private life without further penalties.

5. Peking to remain the capital, Nanking being too much exposed to the preponderating influence of a foreign naval power, and other proposed capitals too inaccessible.

6. No territorial compensation to any foreign Power. Stricter observance of treaties. A money indemnity to be paid, guaranteed on all the revenues of the empire, with the exception of:
(a) Those already hypothecated.
(b) Those necessary to the officials for working expenses.

7. Reorganization of the finances with abolition of all squeezes and sinecures, under European army of occupation, to maintain peace and order until all reforms work smoothly.

8. Limitation of the military and naval forces to be maintained by China, and of the arms and munitions to be imported or manufactured.

9. No forts or camps to be maintained within a radius of thirty miles of the four principal treaty ports, and no forts on waterways navigable by men-of-war. An accurate account shall be kept of all Chinese troops within a radius of thirty miles from any treaty port.

10. Full liberty to Chinese and foreigners to work mines, railways, etc., and navigate inland waters.

11. Missionaries to be restricted to spheres within a radius of thirty miles from a treaty port, female missionaries to be restricted to the treaty ports. No missionary, under pain of punishment or deportation, to engage in anything but the propagation of the Gospel and the spread of knowledge.

12. Proclamations stating the terms of peace to be posted in

every town in China for at least one year, and immediately replaced when destroyed.

It is satisfactory to find that the editor of the English journal takes strong exception to the clause which provides for placing restrictions on missionary enterprise. No man knows better than he that the killing of missionaries was not the cause, but the occasion of the Boxer outbreak—the political jealousy of a foreign dynasty, as well as the objection of a conservative people to every enterprise which appears to take the bread out of their mouths, being really at the bottom of it.[1]

Scarcely would it have been more unfair to accuse missionaries of having caused the *Sepoy* Rebellion than to charge them with provoking the Boxer outrages. In both cases they have been pre-eminently victims rather than parties in the conflict. With the *Sepoy* a greased cartridge was the spark which lighted the explosion; in the case of the Boxers, it was not the blood of the missionary so much as the subsequent manifestation of German aggression and German enterprise, which, as we have said, resulted in their transformation into a great political party.

Missionary societies did not withdraw their agents from India, but felt encouraged to redoubled effort by such statesmen as Lord Lawrence, who declared that missionaries had done more for India than either civilians or military.

In regard to China, not merely has it been occasionally proposed to withdraw missionaries from the interior, but some have even suggested the abandonment of China as a mission field. Such persons are far from understanding the character of the Chinese people. Under a liberal ruler like the young Emperor, they woke up with marvellous suddenness to the wants of their own country, and the superior excellence of our Christian civilization; but under the Empress Dowager, deceived and misguided, they fell in with her reactionary policy. With them it is a fixed principle to follow the guidance of the throne. Often is it asserted in their sacred books that the "One Man," by his teaching and example, is able to lead the nation in the right or the wrong way.

In my mind there remains no doubt that the effects of the recent victory will gradually (for nothing goes fast in China) make a deep impression on the Chinese mind. The effect will be not only a resuscitation of the reform movement, but an adoption of the essential elements of our civilization to an extent never before imagined. The

---

1. His comments, which are worth preserving, may be seen in the Appendix.

way has been cleared for the introduction of a new epoch, which may be expected to commence with the twentieth century.

Glad I am to learn that seventeen missionary societies in America—Baptist, Congregationalist, Episcopal, Methodist, Presbyterian, and some twelve or thirteen others—meeting in convocation recently resolved not to withdraw their missionaries from China, but to make redoubled efforts for the conversion of that populous empire.

They adopted a series of resolutions, of which the following is the substance:

> While the uprising in China has, of course, had a restrictive, and, in some places, a deeply injurious present effect on missionary operations, there is no adequate ground for discouragement, and the work ought to be, and must be, resumed at as early a date as may be practicable and wise. There is no disposition to be reckless in reopening stations. We do not underestimate the possible consequences of premature resumption of work. The servants of the Lord must be sensible, but not for a moment are we discouraged. Clear, strong, and unanimous was the note of both conferences that God will overrule this disturbance for the furtherance of the Gospel: that, just as the most successful era of missionary work in India followed the mutiny of 1857, so will a new day for China date from the Boxer riots of 1900; that not only should every destroyed station be rebuilt, but that plans should be made for reinforcements and increased expenditures, in order that the Church of God may seize the coming strategic opportunity to win China for Christ. The missionaries in particular were united and enthusiastic in the conviction that a large number of new missionaries will be needed next year, and that the young men in the theological seminaries should be encouraged to apply for appointment.

For the whole paper, which acquires immense weight from the fact that it expresses the views of seventeen societies, see Appendix.

The Powers have agreed on the basis of a final settlement. Dr. Morrison, in a cable to the London *Times*, gives the following lucid summary, under date of Peking, Sunday, November 11th. He says:

> Pressed by the common desire for a speedy termination of present conditions, the foreign envoys have finally agreed to the following terms, to be presented in a conjoint note which, subject to the approval of the governments, will be pressed upon

China as the basis of a preliminary treaty:

China shall erect a monument to Baron von Ketteler on the site where he was murdered and send an imperial prince to Germany to convey an apology. She shall inflict the death-penalty upon eleven princes and officials already named, and suspend provincial examinations for five years where the outrages occurred. In future all officials failing to prevent anti-foreign outrages within their jurisdiction shall be dismissed and punished. [This is a modification of Mr. Conger's proposal.]

Indemnity shall be paid to the states, corporations, and individuals. The Tsung Li Yamen shall be abolished, and its functions vested in a foreign minister. Rational intercourse shall be permitted with the Emperor as in civilized countries.

The forts at Taku and the other forts on the coast of Chi-li shall be razed and the importation of arms and war material prohibited. Permanent legation guards shall be maintained, and also guards of communication between Peking and the sea.

Imperial proclamations shall be posted for two years throughout the empire suppressing Boxers.

The indemnity is to include compensation for Chinese who suffered through being employed by foreigners, but not compensation for native Chinese Christians. The words 'missionary' and 'Christian' do not occur in the note.

It is gratifying to know of a certainty that the integrity of China, under her own rulers, is thus provided for. Though nothing is said of the young Emperor, it is understood that if his tyrannical Aunt allows him to return, he will be the figure-head (if nothing more) in the new government, as he has been in the old. Under the new regime, however, the surveillance of the Dowager will be replaced by that of Dame Europa—or better still, that of the two dames, mother and daughter, Europe and America.

That will be sufficient guarantee for a liberal policy which shall make provision for all legitimate interests and enterprises. The open door will be maintained, and, though in this protocol the word missionary does not occur, we refuse to believe that any set of negotiators could be stolid enough to exclude from China the dispensers of knowledge, human and divine; as if light were the one commodity she could afford to dispense with! No such arrangement would be ratified by the Christian World, and if it were, it would not be of long dura-

THE DOWAGER'S PALACE NEAR PEKING

THE EMPRESS DOWAGER OF CHINA

tion; for in a few lustrums a fresh outbreak might be expected which would call for a readjustment of relations on a more liberal basis.

The punishment of the guilty princes commends itself to our sense of justice. The Chinese negotiators pled for their lives, and there was reason to fear they would escape the death-penalty. It would have been an outrage on the moral sense of Christendom to allow Prince Tuan, the great patron of the Boxers, to go with hoary hair down to the grave in peace. Equally abhorrent would it be to permit Prince Chuang, military governor of the city, to come to what the Chinese call Shan Chang, "a happy end," after having issued proclamations setting a price on foreign heads: "*Sixty taels for the head of a man, fifty for the head of a woman, and thirty for the head of a child.*"

As for the Heir Apparent, it would be madness to permit him to ascend the Throne at any future day—especially if his father be condemned to death. For in that case, the first duty incumbent on him would be to avenge his parent. Says the Book of Rites:

"When your father has been slain, wear your sword night and day; and whenever you meet the slayer in palace or in market-place, be ready to plunge it into his bosom."

This passage the Ta Aga will bring to the memory of Christendom, if he be allowed in any way to direct the destinies of the Chinese empire.

A document of scarcely inferior interest to this telegraphic intelligence has just fallen into my hands, *viz.*: the Parliamentary Blue Book, China, No. 3, 1900.

The reports, Consular and Ministerial, which it contains bring us down to the eve of the rupture. Instructive and exciting is the reading which they supply, but on one point only can I allow space for a few extracts, *viz.*: the different aspect which the Boxer movement presented to the eyes of Missionaries and Ministers. As early as January 17th, Sir Claude MacDonald reports to Lord Salisbury that Bishop Scott (after the murder of Mr. Brooks) telegraphed to Mr. Brown to inquire as to the state of affairs, and received on the 9th inst. a reply as follows:

Outlook very black; daily marauding; constant danger. Edict suppressing (Boxers) published. Troops present, but useless; officials complete inaction. Prefect blocks; secret orders from Throne to encourage (Boxers).

On this Sir Claude remarks:

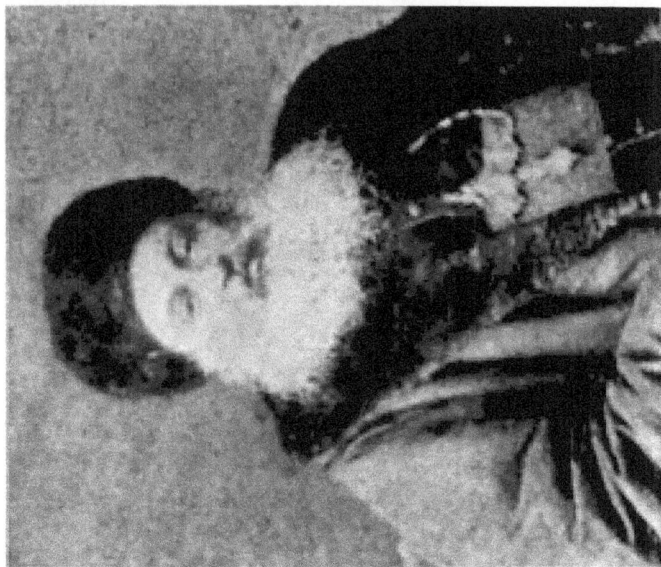

MONSIGNOR FAVIER
CATHOLIC BISHOP OF PEKING

EDWIN H. CONGER
UNITED STATES MINISTER TO CHINA

On the 11th inst. I saw the Ministers of the Tsung Li Yamen and spoke to them in terms of the gravest warning. *While I could not believe it possible, I said, that the rumours of secret orders from the Throne were true.* The mere fact of the currency of such rumours showed the impression which the conduct of the prefect conveyed to the public.

Under date of May 21st H. B. M.'s Minister encloses a letter of Bishop Favier, addressing M. Pichon, as follows:

I beg you will be assured, *Monsieur le Ministre*, that I am well informed, and am making no statements at random. The religious persecution *is only a blind. The main object is to exterminate the Europeans*, and this object is clearly indicated and written on the Boxers' standards.

Commenting on this, Sir Claude says:

It was generally felt (in the diplomatic body) that after making all due *allowances for the colour* which might have been lent to his words by the fears of his converts, his deliberately expressed opinion on the situation could not be treated with indifference. At the same time we did not consider that the circumstances, so far as we were in a position to judge, *were such as to justify the bringing up of Legation Guards.*

Just a week later Sir Claude sends another despatch which is notable as containing the last public utterance of Baron Ketteler. By this time all the Ministers had been waked out of their diplomatic dream by the outrages on the Paoting-fu railway.

During the discussion (in conference) the German Minister declared that it was utterly useless either to expect the Chinese Government to do anything effective, or to take any action ourselves, such as bringing up guards, based on the belief that that Government could remain stable or on the desire to assist in propping *up its crumbling structure.*

That "crumbling structure" has now come to the ground, burying in its ruins the fairest products of foreign enterprise. The Powers have undertaken to set it up again—an undertaking not unlike that of Rome had she resolved to rebuild the city of Pompeii. They may clear away some of the debris, but they can hardly hope for permanence. Nor is the permanence of the structure to be desired unless it give impartial shelter to Christian and to pagan.

The outlook for China is not cheering—even if the Powers join in the maintenance of her territorial integrity—yet is it far from hopeless.

The views of Sir Robert Hart, as given in the *Fortnightly*, are a little too pessimistic. He thinks (and his opinions are not to be lightly disregarded) that the Boxer craze will continue to spread; that within two or three years there will be in China twenty million Boxers; and that there is but one cure for it, *viz.*: the rapid spread of Christianity—but of that he sees no hope.

In two points out of three my views are in accord with his, but I do not share his gloomy anticipations.

The defeat of the power that called the Boxers out of their obscure retreat is almost certain to be followed by a collapse of the Boxers—especially as the Chinese public holds them responsible for the calamities the Empress Dowager has brought on the empire. She herself makes them her scapegoat; nor does she appear inclined to let them go unscathed, as the Hebrews did with their vicarious victim. Even now their tide is on the ebb, and in a few months it may be that nothing will remain of the disastrous flood but here and there a brackish pool. That Christianity is the most radical, if not the sole, remedy for this curse of pagan fanaticism, I firmly believe. That its spread cannot, in the nature of the case, be as rapid as that of the Boxers, I also admit. Yet do the fires kindled by the Boxers throw light on the success of missions, and prove that Christianity *was* making no little headway.

TEMPLE OF HEAVEN IN PEKING, OCCUPIED AS A CAMP BY BRITISH SOLDIERS

Appendix

Note.—The three poems which follow are in themselves full of interest. Translated by the author, and now published for the first time in this country, they throw much light on Chinese life. One expressing conjugal tenderness, another showing that China has her heroines, and a third proving that the Chinese are not devoid of chivalrous sentiment. People capable of this strain of feeling are not beyond the pale of our sympathy.

Of the three prose documents it is enough to say that they are cited in the text as of great value.

Su Wu to His Wife

On Setting Out on His Embassy to the Court of the Grand Khan of Tartary, 100 B.C.[1]

Twin trees whose boughs together twine,
Two birds that guard one nest,
We'll soon be far asunder torn,
As sunrise from the west.

Hearts knit in childhood's innocence,
Long bound in Hymen's ties;
One goes to distant battle-fields,
One sits at home and sighs.

Like carrier bird, though seas divide,
I'll seek my lonely mate;

---

1. On arriving he was thrown into prison, lowered into a well, and treated with great indignity. We are not told that his life was threatened, yet his master made war on the *Khan* to rescue or avenge him. The *Khan* in great alarm released him and came to terms. With such precedents in their history how could the Dowager and her clique be so blind as to follow the example of the Grand *Khan*?

But if afar I find a grave,
You'll mourn my hapless fate.

To us the future's all unknown,
In memory seek relief;
Come, touch the chords you know so well,
And let them soothe our grief.

MULAN, A CHINESE JOAN OF ARC

A Chinese Ballad of the Liang Dynasty, 502–556 a.d.

An officer being disabled, his daughter puts on his armour, and, so disguised, leads his troops to the conflict. The original is anonymous and of uncertain date.

Say, maiden, at your spinning-wheel,
Why heave that deep-drawn sigh?
Is't fear perchance or love you feel,
Pray tell—oh, tell me why?

Nor fear nor love has moved my soul—
Away such idle thought!
A warrior's glory is the goal
By my ambition sought.

My father's cherished life to save,
My country to redeem,
The dangers of the field I'll brave—
I am not what I seem.

No son has he his troop to lead,
No brother dear have I;
So I must mount my father's steed,
And to the battle hie.

At dawn of day she quits her door,
At evening rests her head
Where loud the mountain torrents roar
And mail-clad soldiers tread.

The northern plains are gained at last,
The mountains sink from view,
The sun shines cold, and the wintry blast
It pierces through and through.

A thousand foes around her fall,
And red blood stains the ground;

But Mulan, who survives it all,
Returns with glory crowned.

Before the throne they bend the knee,
In the palace of Chang-an,
Full many a knight of high degree,
But the bravest is Mulan.

Nay, Prince, she cries, my duty's done,
No guerdon I desire,
But let me to my home begone,
To cheer my aged sire.

She nears the door of her father's home,
A chief with trumpet's blare,
But when she doffs her waving plume,
She stands a maiden fair.

THE MIDNIGHT OFFERING

A Tale of the Tartar Wars, Related by a Manchu of the Imperial Clan.

On the last night of the year the Emperor offers a sacrifice in one of his family temples on the east of the canal, not far from the British Legation, and it is generally believed that this sacrifice is offered, in whole or in part, to the manes of a Chinese general, who, nearly three centuries ago, opposed the advance of the Tartars.

You ask me to tell why, in yonder halls,
The Lord of the Rivers and Hills
There at midnight low on the pavement falls,
And an annual rite fulfils.

'Twas after the rise of our Manchu clan,
When our sires were roaming the plains,
This rite was ordained for a worthy man,
Whose honour unfading remains.

One morning our Founder, the brave Tai-tsu,
Was beat in a terrible fight;
His arrows were spent, his spear broke in two,
And safety lay only in flight

The cloud of pursuers waxed thin and few,
As through the thick jungle he sped;
One warrior at last left alone to pursue,
And fleeter the fugitive fled.

110

All way-worn and weary, but not in despair,
He sought in the jungle to hide;
Only hoping at best for a wild beast's lair,
When a vine-covered cavern he spied.

My lady! he cried to an aged crone,
Whom at the cave's entrance he found,
Pray let me repose in your fortress of stone,
And spread me a mat on the ground.

Refreshment and shelter I will not withhold;
You've nothing to fear, said the dame,
For I have a son, who's a soldier bold;
In his need I should wish him the same.

Just then the pursuer burst into the cave,
The flash of his falchion was seen;
But, thoughtful the life of her stranger to save,
The matron quick rushed in between.

Spare the life of my guest, and touch not a hair;
I received him for your sake alone!—
For your sake, my mother, the stranger I spare,
But you've bartered the life of your son.

For you have I broken my chieftain's command,
My blood must atone for my guilt;
So saying, the blade that he held in his hand
He plunged in his heart to the hilt

Farewell, Noble Soul! the brave Tai-tsu exclaimed.
My brother! your mother is mine.
In ages to come, you'll with honour be named
And adored in our family shrine.

FUTURE MISSIONARY POLICY IN CHINA
A NOTABLE CONFERENCE OF MISSIONARY SECRETARIES.

By Rev. Arthur J. Brown, D.D., New York City. Secretary of the Presbyterian Board for Foreign Missions.

Now that immediate danger of the further destruction of missionary life in China has probably passed, stupendous problems of reconstruction confront us. Never before in all the history of missions have such difficult and delicate questions called for an answer. The work of the largest mission field in the world is paralyzed, many stations have been abandoned, and the missionaries are fugitives in the port cities, and in Korea and Japan, while at home the expediency of the whole missionary enterprise is being challenged, the boards are urged to send no more missionaries to China, and some people frankly say that in any event they will give no more money for missionary work in China.

In these circumstances every board has a heavy responsibility. In order that we in the Presbyterian Board might have sound counsel, we first sought the opinions of the missionaries themselves. So we cabled to those assembled in Chefoo, asking them to hold a meeting, consider the policy that ought to be adopted, and wire us their judgment. Providentially, there were about forty Presbyterian missionaries from China in this country on furlough. We selected eight wise, devoted men, representing all our missions in China, brought them to New York at the expense of the board, and spent many profitable hours with them, listening to all that was in their hearts, after the months of thought and prayer which they had naturally given to the subject. Nor was this all, for we wrote to all the other missionaries from China now in the United States, explaining that while it was impracticable for financial reasons to bring so many to New York, yet we desired their opinions too, and requesting each one to freely write any suggestions. Thus we did everything in our power to ascertain the views of the devoted missionaries themselves.

Realizing, however, that the questions before us were common to other boards similarly situated, all the boards of foreign missions in the United States and Canada, having work in China, were invited to send delegates to an interdenominational conference in New York. The invitation was cordially accepted, and September 21 thirty-two delegates assembled in our board rooms, representing nearly all the leading Protestant bodies of America. In this conference also the entire ground was traversed, step by step, including a docket embracing thirty topics and sub-topics. The conference was of extraordinary interest and value. While the discussions were free and the opinions not always unanimous, yet harmony prevailed to a remarkable degree. The session began with a season of special prayer for Divine guidance, and never was prayer more plainly answered. We separated, feeling that we had been greatly helped, that our vision had been clarified, and that we were prepared to submit clearer judgment to our respective boards.

The main lines of policy agreed upon by both missionaries and board representatives (for with one minor exception practically identical views were expressed in the two conferences), and which will now be voted upon by the boards concerned were as follows:

RESUMPTION OF THE WORK

1. While the uprising in China has, of course, had a restrictive, and in some places a deeply injurious present effect on missionary operations, there is no adequate ground for discouragement, and the work ought to be, and must be resumed at as early a date as may be practicable and wise. There is no disposition to be reckless in reopening stations. We do not underestimate the possible consequences of premature resumption of work. The servants of the Lord must be sensible. But not for a moment are we discouraged. Clear, strong, and unanimous was the note of both conferences that God will overrule this disturbance for the furtherance of the Gospel, that just as the most successful era of missionary work in India followed the mutiny of 1857, so will a new day for China date from the Boxer riots of 1900; that not only should every destroyed station be rebuilt, but that plans should be made for re-enforcements and increased expenditures, in order that the Church of God may seize the coming strategic opportunity to win China for Christ. The missionaries in particular were united and enthusiastic in the conviction that a large number of new missionaries will be needed next year, and that the young men in the theological seminaries should be encouraged to apply for appointment.

AN AGGRESSIVE POLICY AT HOME

2. In view of the public interest in China, the frequent denial of the validity of the whole missionary enterprise, and the fact that the missionary cause now has the attention of the country as never before, it was unanimously agreed that we should adopt an aggressive policy at home. A committee was therefore appointed to prepare a joint letter to the American churches, reaffirming the Divine authority of missions as of supreme and perpetual obligation, emphasizing the true significance of the present situation in China, and summoning the churches to special gifts for the re-establishment and enlargement of the work, and to the observance of the week beginning October 28th, as *a week of special prayer*, with memorial services for martyred missionaries.

It was also voted that the letter should include reference to the noble fidelity of the Chinese Christians under the awful persecution to which they have been subjected, com- mend them to the sympathies and prayers of God's people everywhere, and heartily indorse the appeal of Minister Conger and representative missionaries in Peking, for relief contributions, the conference holding that these Christians were worthy of a generosity similar to that which has been extended to the famine sufferers in India. We hope that this letter will be read from every pulpit in the United States and Canada, and made the subject of Sabbath sermons, midweek devotional meetings, family prayers, and such other services as may be deemed advisable by the pastors concerned.

The Missionaries Now in China

3. Sympathetic consideration was given to the embarrassment of the missionaries who are crowded in the port cities, with only the scanty clothing they happened to be wearing when they fled from their stations, and forced to pay high prices for rent and supplies. Is the interruption of work likely to be so long continued that they should come home? Both furloughed missionaries and board representatives felt that a general recall to America was neither necessary nor expedient. Such a return would involve an enormous expense, for our Presbyterian Board alone has over 150 China missionaries still abroad. It would destroy the continuity of the work, leave the Chinese Christians to unrelieved suffering and disaster, and the remaining mission property to be still further damaged.

It would make it impossible to resume the work if, in the providence of God, such resumption should be practicable within a few months. The home church would be unfavourably affected by such a general withdrawal, naturally construing it as an admission of defeat, and indefinite postponement of missionary work, and in consequence diminishing gifts, while as the usual term of service in China is about eight years, so many furloughs now would mean that eight or nine years hence most of the missionaries in China would need a furlough, and so another general exodus would be necessary, thus practically subjecting the work for an indefinite period to alternations of vigorous effort, and more or less complete inaction.

All agreed therefore that, except where conditions of ill health or nervous strain render an immediate return necessary, the missionaries now on the field should await developments in Korea, Japan, and such China ports as may be safe, in anticipation of an early resumption of the work, the care and reconstruction of the mission property, and particularly the guidance and comfort of the Chinese Christians, who otherwise would be left to the wolves as sheep having no shepherd. The suggestion was made that missionaries who may not be able to return to their own stations might temporarily assist other stations or missions.

In like manner, there was general agreement that while each board must determine for itself when missionaries on furlough and new missionaries under appointment should leave for their respective fields, such missionaries should not anticipate an indefinite delay in this country, but should hold themselves in readiness to sail at such dates as might prove practicable in consultation with their respective boards. Some of these rested, vigorous men may be needed at once to relieve their North China brethren who have been exhausted by the awful experiences of recent months.

The Question of Indemnity

4. Much time was given to the question of indemnity. Eight boards reported definite knowledge of destroyed or damaged property, in some instances to a very large amount, while most of the other boards anticipated losses. Not all saw alike on this question. There was, however, unanimity in the conviction that it would be highly unbecoming in the followers of Christ to manifest a mercenary spirit and make exorbitant demands upon the Chinese, especially as corrupt officials would probably squeeze the required sums out of the innocent villagers, and count themselves lucky in getting off so easy. After full discussion, vote was taken upon the motion that: *(a)* When the governments shall ask for information as to claims for indemnity, such claims should not include suffering, loss of life, or interruption of work, but only the actual value of destroyed or injured property, and the extraordinary expenses incurred in consequence of the troubles, and *(b)* in exceptional cases, for loss of life which has destroyed the means of support for wife and children.

The question being divided, *(a)* was carried unanimously, though one delegate did not vote. On *(b)* a majority held that in such cases a claim might reasonably be made on behalf of an otherwise destitute family, though a minority felt that not even then should a money value be placed on missionary life, and that the care of dependent relatives was a proper charge on the home church. It was unanimously voted that claims for indemnity should not be presented by individual missionaries directly to the civil authorities, but only through their respective boards, and that it was inexpedient to appoint an interdenominational committee to collate and present these claims, but that each board should act for itself.

The thought here was not to interfere with the liberty of any missionary, but rather to relieve him and also the government. Several hundred missionaries are involved. They are widely scattered. While a few are so situated that they might effectively push their own claims, a large majority would be under great disadvantage in conducting the necessary negotiations. Nor must we forget the embarrassment to which our government might be exposed. The State Department has been exceedingly kind, and no member of the administration has ever even hinted at the annoyance of which Lord Salisbury complained in England. Nevertheless, we can readily see what delicacies would be involved if so many individuals were to be pushing indemnity claims with varying degrees of vigour and with widely different ideas as to what objects should be included.

Moreover, experience with Oriental governments hardly justifies the belief that the indemnity will be paid within ten days! While the negotiations are pending, how are the missionaries to be carried? They must have immediate reimbursement for the extraordinary expense which they have incurred. Manifestly the boards must stand behind the missionaries, promptly meeting their necessary and pressing obligations, and then deal with the government regarding the indemnity. The boards are better able to bear the burden of delay than the individual missionaries. In the Presbyterian Board we shall follow the analogy of our annual estimates, ask each individual and station to make out a schedule, have it voted on by the mission, and then forwarded to the board in New York. In this way the vexed question of indemnity can be handled in an orderly and prudent manner. We shall avoid demands which might subject the whole missionary enterprise to criticism, and we shall not embitter the Chinese by taking what might be deemed unfair advantage of them.

MISSIONARIES AND THE CIVIL POWERS

5. The conference was not disposed to allow critics to define the relation of the missionary to the civil power, especially as those critics do not ordinarily distinguish between the radically different practises of Roman Catholics and Protestants. It was felt that this would be a good time for the Protestant missionary bodies to put themselves on record. As such a paper could not wisely be framed amid the hurry of a conference, a committee was appointed to draft it, and to report at the annual joint conference next January. Meantime, the Presbyterian missionaries unanimously declared it to be their rule not to apply to the civil authorities unless absolutely necessary, and that they had repeatedly refused to make such appeals when they might reasonably have done so.

The Rev. Dr. A. A. Fulton, of Canton, stated that he had not appealed to the civil authorities half a dozen times in twenty years. The Rev. A. M. Cunningham, of Peking, had appealed only twice in eight and a half years, and then simply to transmit information; the Rev w P. W. McClintock, of Hainan, only once in eight years; the Rev. Dr. J. N. Hayes, of Suchou, once in eighteen years; the Rev. J. H. Laughlin, of Shantung, never in nineteen years. And the missionaries stated that they believed themselves to be fairly representative of the practice of American Protestant missionaries in China.

A significant indication of the attitude of the boards was given in the vote on a request that had been cabled from China to several boards, asking them to protest to Washington against the proposed evacuation of Peking by the allied armies and the reinstatement of the Empress-dowager, as disastrous to missions. Some of the missionaries thought that such a protest should be made on the ground that the withdrawal of the armies and the reinstatement of the Empress would be construed by the Chinese as a victory for them, destroy the moral effect of the occupation of Peking, and perhaps lead to the renewal of trouble. The interdenominational conference, however, unanimously voted to take no action.

Some of its members had decided convictions as to what the governments ought to do; but they held that it was not proper for missionary workers, as such, to proffer unasked advice to the government in a matter so distinctly within its sphere, nor were they willing to go on record as saying that an armed force is necessary to missionary interests anywhere. While several of the missionaries felt that the instigators and leaders of the uprising should be punished in the interest of future security, the majority declared that this question also belonged to the government, which was understood to have it under consideration, and that any demand on the part of missionaries or boards was to be seriously deprecated. The power of the sword has not been committed to us, and the civil magistrate to whom it has been committed should, in our judgment, exercise that power on his own initiative and responsibility.

On May 15, the Presbyterian Board adopted a declaration of principles of comity, and expressed to its sister boards its cordial willingness to co-operate in any practical measures to carry them into effect. The suggestion was made that a providential opportunity had now occurred. Manifestly the conference could not take final action on such a question, but it unanimously adopted the following resolution:

> It is the judgment of this conference that the resumption of mission work in those parts of China where it has been interrupted would afford a favourable opportunity for putting into practise some of the principles of mission comity which have been approved by a general consensus of opinion among missionaries and boards, especially in regard to the overlapping of fields and such work as printing and publishing, higher education and hospital work, and the conference would commend the subject to the favourable consideration and action of the various boards and their missionaries.

Each board will immediately inaugurate a vigorous foreign missionary campaign among the home churches. In the Presbyterian Board, we are urging the missionaries from China now in this country to avail themselves of the public interest by freely contributing articles to the religious and secular papers, and to give all practicable time to the home department secretary for addresses. We are calling upon the churches not only to maintain their usual gifts, but to provide a large fund with which we can meet the extraordinary expenses incurred during recent months, and in due time rebuild the ruined stations and enlarge the work.

We propose to divide this estimated special expenditure into shares of one hundred dollars each, and endeavour to place them with churches, societies, and individuals, such shares to be in excess of ordinary contributions and of the fifteen *per cent*, increase required for the maintenance of the regular work. It will thus be seen that the steady tone of both conferences was distinctively hopeful. All felt that the American churches are now being brought into new relations with the unevangelized races. They must no longer regard foreign missions as simply one of many causes calling for collections, but be led to recognize the world-wide preaching of the Gospel as the great work for which the Church is set. May we not confidently rely upon the prayers of all the friends of missions as we now summon the churches to go forward in the name of the Lord of Hosts?

THE MARTYRED MISSIONARIES

Very tender was that part of the conference in which report was made of martyrdoms. Only two boards represented were thus bereaved, but they have lost heavily. The American Board announced the massacre of one man and two women at Pao-ting-fu and the entire Shansi force—five men, five women, and five children. The Presbyterian board mourns the death of three men, two women, and three children at Pao-ting-fu—a total for both boards of eighteen missionaries and eight little ones. Considering the large number of American missionaries in China, and the magnitude and violence of the outbreak, this is a comparatively small numerical loss. But when we add the European missionaries who also ascended in that tumult of fire, the list lengthens to appalling proportions.

None who knew them can scan that roll of martyrs without feeling that the soil of China has been forever consecrated by the blood of God's saints—"of whom the world was not worthy." May God show the shining of His face through the cloud of sorrow, and may He grant to those who remain a new spirit of love and power for the Master who Himself tasted the bitterness of death for us all!

SIR ROBERT HART

SOME COLLEGE MEMORIES

The Belfast Northern Whig of the 21st of July has the following interesting letter from the president of Queen's College, Belfast:

To the Editor of the *Northern Whig*,

Sir—With a heavy heart I sit down to ask your permission to weave if only a little chaplet for the bier of my friend, Sir Robert Hart, whose terrible death you chronicle for us today.

Were this college in session, and not, as it is, in the midst of the long vacation, I have no doubt an official pronouncement would be made testifying to the unutterable regret which I know is felt throughout our entire body at the awful news. As it is, I can only speak feebly for myself what would otherwise be said much more effectively, and with all the weight of authority, by the College Council. The death is, I need not say, an irreparable loss to our empire and to the cause of civilization and progress all over the world. But to Queen's College, Belfast, it is a personal bereavement. Sir Robert Hart was one of our earliest alumni, and we were all proud of him with a pardonable pride. It is sad to turn now to our "Calendar," as I have done this morning, and read of his career, when, in the early flush of ambition, he trod our cloisters with Reichel, and MacDouall and Craik, and Andrews and M'Cosh, and the other professors of that day, and contended for our scholarships and prizes with fellow- students, too many of whom are also, alas! no more.

It was in 1850 that he entered college. His form of application for admission, filled up in his own youthful handwriting, is preserved among the archives in the Registrar's office, and is now a precious relic. In his first year he won a junior literary scholarship in the Faculty of Arts. Next year he gained another, one of his competitors, who ran him very close, and in the end took a higher place, being James Cuming, who was in later years to become our widely known professor of medicine.

In 1852 he took a third-year scholarship, this time topping the list, and next year he crowned his career among us by gaining the highest honour then in our gift—a senior scholarship—his subjects for which were modern languages and modern history. He then graduated, not, as has been stated, in the University of Dublin, but, of course, in the old Queen's University, and took first honours in two groups of subjects—English and logic and metaphysics. Not long after, on the advice, I believe, of Dr. Andrews and Dr. M'Cosh, he entered on that career from which China was to reap such splendid fruit, and which has now ended so tragically. Ever since his course has been watched with—may I not say?—a unique and admiring interest, and ever since also he has proved himself the fast friend of his old college. To student after student he opened careers in China.

Mr. S. M. Russell, who, it is to be feared, has now shared his fate, and Mr. C. H. Oliver were appointed through him professors in the Imperial College, Peking, and other men were given posts in the Imperial Maritime Customs which Sir Robert may be said to have created. Today there are specially recalled to my memory two little incidents in the recent history of our college—little but significant—in which his love for his Alma Mater shone out conspicuously. Eight years ago I wrote him of the proposal to establish a Students' Union here, and by next post came, not only his cheque for £200, but a letter, warmly approving of the project and breathing the most ardent affection for the scene of his early studies and academic struggles. The other incident occurred when, a few years later, we celebrated the jubilee of the college. He then sent me another letter, the reading of which at the memorable meeting in our library, in the presence of the Lord Lieutenant and the many other notable personages who honoured us with their presence that day, was not the least interesting feature of a remarkable occasion. In it he regretted keenly that he could not be with us to share our joy and join in our congratulations, and recalled many interesting details of his student days.

It is unutterably saddening to think that that busy brain and that warm heart are now for ever still. In the terribly long list of deaths which this year has brought—deaths which have tolled and are still tolling their muffled knells in our hearts—his stands out in melancholy prominence. But the great work which he has done remains behind, and it will be long indeed before the illustrious name, the splendid services to humanity, and the unsullied reputation of Robert Hart pass into oblivion.

Thomas Hamilton.
Queen's College, Belfast, July 16, 1900.

English Comments on German Scheme
From The North China Herald.[2]

Some of the above conditions will commend themselves to those charged with the negotiation of peace with China. Some are impracticable or unadvisable. No. 1 is all right. As to No. 2, the first part is all right; as to the second part, whoever negotiates with the Chinese, whether one person or more, must be the mouthpiece of a conference of the Powers, who will all want to be heard, and few of whom are likely to be willing to intrust their interests entirely to others. Nos. 3 and 4 are all right. As to No. 5, if Nanking is too much exposed to the preponderating influence of a foreign naval Power, Peking is equally exposed to the preponderating influence of a foreign military Power. There is a little jealousy about the objection to Nanking, but that is another story. Nanking is certainly in every way preferable as capital to Peking. No. 6 is all right. No. 7 is all right if the European control of the finances of China takes the form of an international service like the Imperial Maritime Customs.

2. See Chapter 8

A European army of occupation will no doubt be necessary for a time, but if the settlement is to be permanent and to work smoothly the Chinese must not be humiliated more than is absolutely necessary. This objection applies also to Nos. 8 and 9; it is not desirable to try and impose terms which China would rather fight to the death than accept. Men like Liu Kun-yi and Chang Chih-tung must be considered; and we cannot imagine their acceding, under the circumstances, to such terms as these.

No. 10 is all right; but what knowledge should we have of the interior of China now if such a regulation as No. 11 had been always in force? We would certainly approve of a restriction on the presence of unmarried foreign women in the interior; but we cannot see that a missionary has any less right to go outside thirty miles from a treaty port than a trader or an engineer. No. 11 seems to us both impracticable and unadvisable. No. 12 is all right. While we do not agree with all these suggestions, we think their publication is eminently desirable; the more those who know China well publish their conceptions of the terms that should be exacted, and the more these are discussed, the easier it will be for the negotiators when the time comes to arrive at a satisfactory result.